UNDER THE CROSS

UNDER THE CROSS
STUDIES IN THE CHURCH'S MISSION TODAY

JEAN M. FRASER

Jean Fraser

EDINBURGH HOUSE PRESS
2 EATON GATE, LONDON, S.W.1

First published 1956

Printed by Wm. Carling & Co. Ltd., London & Hitchin

CONTENTS

CONTENTS

FOREWORD

In a village church on the outskirts of an English town is a modern rood-screen. The side facing the people shows the out-reaching of the love of God to men. Christ hangs on the Cross but his eyes are looking out in love to the world. The figures on the uprights show how God has sought men, through the prophets of the Old Testament, the Apostles of the New, and the missionaries who brought the Gospel to these islands. Along the great beam run the tendrils of the Vine, symbol of the Church, which springs from the foot of the Cross and bears as its fruits the Sacraments represented as God's gifts for human life.

On the East side, Christ reigns from the Cross and the great beam and the uprights express the worship of the whole creation and the angelic host as they acknowledge him Lord and King.

This is the sense in which we understand "the Church under the Cross". It is the Church which shares, to the point of suffering and sacrifice, Christ's outgoing love to all the world. It is a Church which often presents to the world a figure as little glorious and "successful" as were the three crosses on the hill. But in its life and worship it holds fast to the faith that the Christ who was put to death on Calvary is the Lord who reigns over heaven and earth, "whom angels praise and saints adore", and who will one day "take his power and reign".

In a particular sense also the Church in our day is "under the Cross", especially as it seeks to become universal in fact as well as in faith. The Cross can be seen as the point of inter-section of time and eternity, the symbol of God made man. The Church too is human and divine, but while Christ was perfect man the

Church is but a community of redeemed sinners. So we find in our own day the dilemma and perplexity which arise when its best efforts seem to produce evil as well as good results, and when many of its best intentions are misinterpreted.

The "missionary century" that is just over has its glorious achievement in the growth of churches all over the world. Yet this has brought us to a point of transition and adjustment which is painful on both sides. This book does not seek to be "wise after the event", for things could scarcely have happened otherwise, but it does believe that we must not be blind to what is happening now, nor discouraged by it. It emphasises the side of the Cross which is towards the world. It remembers that Jesus did not expect that the world would receive the Church in any other way than it received Him. But it does not forget the Eastward looking side of the rood-screen and the confidence and hope that that inspires.

8

I

"This shall never happen to you!"

"... Jesus began to show his disciples that he must go to Jerusalem and suffer many things ... and be killed and on the third day be raised. And Peter took him and began to rebuke him, saying, 'God forbid Lord! This shall never happen to you.' " (Matt. 16 : 22)

The disciples had just lived through one of their greatest moments. Jesus had put the direct question: "Whom say ye that I am?" Peter, perhaps with sudden insight, perhaps after long reflexion, had answered, "Thou art the Christ, the Son of the Living God." And Jesus had answered his confession by committing to him the authority which Jesus himself exercised.

Jesus now felt that the disciples were fully prepared to share with him what was to come and for the first time he entrusted to them his own knowledge of the Cross that awaited him in Jerusalem. But this was more than Peter could bear. This was not what he had in mind when he called Jesus the Christ. This was not what he understood by holding the keys of heaven. He took Jesus and began to rebuke him, saying, "God forbid, Lord! This shall never happen to you."

Perhaps this dismay is a little the mood of the Church at the present time. We had thought that the missionary movement was going on from triumph to triumph and instead it seems to have struck trouble. We had expected that opposition would have been left behind with the early pioneering days. Instead it seems to rear its head where we thought the work was most secure. Jesus' reply to Peter: "Your outlook is not God's but man's"

9

(Moffat's translation) is perhaps a reminder to us that we have allowed human standards of success and failure to colour our thoughts about the work of Christ in the world. Jesus is sure only of the Cross.

THE other day I bought a map of the world in an Edinburgh book shop. I opened it up and my finger instinctively went to the centre to rest on Great Britain. Instead, it rested on the Pacific Ocean, for the modern map of the world shows two great land masses facing each other—that of Asia on the West and the Americas on the East. Europe is just the Westernmost outpost of that Western landmass.

The map is one illustration of the tremendous changes that have taken place in the last twenty years. Here is another way in which it came home to me, looking back over the ecumenical conferences of recent years.

In 1939 at the first World Conference of Christian Youth the only Germans who were present were there *incognito*—and some of them never returned to Germany. Difficult discussions took place between the British and the Indian delegates, for the Indians were in the midst of the struggle for independence and were bitterly accusing Britain of failing to fulfil her pledges. Two weeks after the end of the Conference the Second World War broke out.

In 1947, the Second World Conference of Christian Youth was held. The Germans were there this time, but it had taken endless negotiation before the Norwegian Government agreed to risk their presence in a country so lately occupied by them as enemies. The Japanese were absent, for on the quayside waiting to board their ship, they learnt that their permits from the occupying authorities to leave Japan had been refused. The difficult discussions, going on long into the night, were this time between Dutch and Indonesians, for they were in the midst of a war for independence. The Philippinos were celebrating their freedom from Colonial rule. The Burmese heard with grief and dismay of the murder of six members of the Cabinet which was to have brought independence to their country. Only a strong sense that God had brought them to the Conference kept them from returning immediately to their country, for these young Cabinet Ministers were their friends. While we were at the Conference the independence of India was declared, and the national flag proudly hoisted.

Three years later, a Central Committee of the World Council of Churches at Toronto expressed its support for the United Nations' action in resisting the Communist aggression in Korea. This declaration brought strong protest from the member churches in Czechoslovakia, Hungary and China, none of which countries was able to send representatives, for since 1947 all had come under Communist control.

The year 1952 saw the Third World Conference of Christian Youth meeting in India—the first World Christian meeting at which the great majority of delegates came from the Asian countries. The Chinese and Eastern Europeans were absent, but six Asian nations were represented which had gained their independence since the end of the War—India, Pakistan, Burma, Ceylon, the Philippines, and Indonesia. No wonder the Conference rejoiced in facing "world problems in an Asian setting".

By the time of the Second Assembly of the World Council of Churches in 1954, the temper of the times had changed again so that some at least of the churches in Communist countries were able to send delegates, who made a big contribution. While Asia was well represented, the new arrival on the scene was Africa, speaking for herself and playing a full part. There was also a larger and more representative group from the Orthodox churches, East and West.

And in the summer of 1955 the Church leaders from the Soviet Union began to make the first visits to churches of other countries since before the 1917 revolution. . . .

The revolution that has taken place is not just a Communist revolution or an Asian revolution. It affects the whole world. Six nations do not gain their independence without affecting the countries which once governed them. China does not become Communist until there has been a revolution in Eastern Europe. Africa, which is still with certain exceptions under European control, watches eagerly every step that is taken in Asia, for she is determined also to take her destiny into her own hands.

The map has become a world map, not a map of Europe and outlying territories.

What happens to the Nations affects the Churches. It affects them because their members are citizens, sharing the joys and travail of their nation. It affects them even more directly as organised bodies, often adversely. Here surely is part of the meaning of the Cross for the Church to-day. Independence in almost every case has meant trouble for the Christian minorities. In Burma, the strength of the Christian community is among the hill peoples, racially distinct from the Burmans. So in the Karen insurrection which for years disrupted Burma after the achievement of independence, it was temptingly easy to identify Christians with the insurrectionists (indeed some Christians were involved) and to look upon them as politically unreliable. In India, the removal of British rule, with its reputation for impartial justice, has opened the way in certain places, especially in rural areas, for an aggressive Hinduism which has found means to stop access of Christians to the village well, which has discriminated against them in educational opportunity and made them the victims of petty persecution. The recent decision of Pakistan, after many years without a Constitution, to become a Muslim state, means that *all* minorities, not only Christians, may be treated as second class citizens, restricted as to employment, with Government service practically closed to them and the stigma of divided loyalty attached to them. And in the South Sudan, where an arbitrarily drawn frontier includes the territory of tribal Africans, Christian and pagan, racially distinct from the Muslims, there is considerable fear that political independence and Moslem rule will be greatly to their disadvantage.

Yet one cannot wish the political clock to be put back in order to protect the Christians, and they themselves would not ask for it. Nor must we too quickly feel Christian indignation if changed relations between States affect freedom of travel and perhaps raise difficulties in the granting of visas. If we believe that the world as well as the Church is in God's hands, that the Church is in the world to bring the nations, as well as individuals, into the kingdom, then we must try to see the will of God and the wisdom of God also in political change. If this means the way of the Cross for churches which are still young in history, we must stand by them in prayer, in protest if need be. Above all, we must stand by them in the faith that God has not abandoned them, but has tasks for them to do in this situation, which may help to determine the character and quality of the life of these new nations.

What this new day means in Asia can be seen in a recently published book, *Christianity and the Asian Revolution*.[1] In its opening paragraph it says:—

"Half a century ago only a handful of foreign troops were required to suppress the Boxer Rebellion and to impose Western terms on China. To-day the armies of sixteen nations, including some of the most powerful in the world, have been stalemated in Korea by the new Chinese army. In 1943 Winston Churchill proclaimed, 'I did not become His Majesty's Prime Minister to preside over the liquidation of the British Empire.' To-day, India, Pakistan, Burma, Ceylon, Indonesia, and the Philippines are independent nations. In recent years the white man had a privileged position in Asia, and many fashionable clubs were reserved exclusively for Europeans. To-day the theory of white racial superiority is thoroughly discredited, and Europeans are welcome in most of Asia only as friends and equals."

[1] Edited by R. B. Manikam, C.L.S. Madras.

Every man holds his head higher when he knows he is a member of an independent nation, even though political freedom is the beginning rather than the end of many problems. Asians hold their heads particularly high because, in all the countries mentioned above except Indonesia, independence was won without armed conflict.

National pride also means that everything which specifically belongs to one's nation—its languages, customs, art, history, religion, traditions, many of which have been forgotten, suppressed or discouraged during colonial days—come to have new significance. Everything which recalls the previous régime is at a discount. Minority groups are likely to be specially sensitive on this score, because they want to show that they are making common cause with their nation, that they have a place in the new order and are not out of step nor hangers-on of the old régime.

This sense of independence of status and judgment inevitably brings with it much criticism of Europe and the West. This is of course first directed against imperialism and expresses the resentment of Asian countries against the governing powers' habit of exploiting raw materials and cheap labour, without encouraging the industrial development which could raise the standard of living. Asia and Africa became, they believed, the "proletariat" of the West.

But more radically, they criticise Western assumptions of racial and cultural superiority, and question Western institutions, the Western way of life, and the Western religion. If all this leads to disastrous wars, in which Asians are involved without their consent having been sought, if Europe remains divided into tiny nation states while great countries covering vast areas like India, Indonesia, or China can act as one unit—then maybe it is time for Asia to show the way. Nehru is quoted in the daily press of September 18th, 1955, as saying in Delhi: "In these times of difficulty, India has played a significant rôle in spreading the ideas of peaceful co-existence and peaceful settlement and, above all, of non-interference in others countries' affairs." And a spokesman for the Buddhist World Council claims for it the credit for "the cooling off of the temper of war through the peaceful thoughts which have radiated throughout the world from the Buddhist Assembly."

Naturally this new nationalism looks askance at "foreign missionary activity", especially when many of the missionaries are of the same nation as the political power which they have just thrown off.

When we in the West write the history of missions, we are careful to show that the picture of the missionary as the running dog of the imperialists is a false one, that missionaries have not slavishly followed the flag but have frequently been in conflict with their own Governments in going into new countries. In India they also have it to their credit that no missionary left India because of the political change. All that may be accurate, but for the moment it carries little weight. As far as Asia and Africa are concerned, the missionary comes from the West and so does imperialism. Both have white skins, and in any time of physical danger, missionaries are protected by their own Government's representatives. They remind the new nations of the old days.

This perhaps puts in a different light the recent action of the Indian Government in taking powers to control the entry of missionaries from Commonwealth as well as non-Commonwealth countries. Many Indian Christians would sympathise with the view that foreigners should not be appointed, in any sphere, to posts which could be filled by Indians. They feel that there have been times when missionaries have held on to posts too long —that the transfer of responsibility has not gone on as fast in the Church as it has in business and government. Whereas the missionary bodies in the West are aware how much has been accomplished, there are elements in the Indian church which are more inclined to dwell on what remains to be done!

Not only is the missionary from the West, but he bears stamped on him, together with the brand of Christ, the brand of every Westerner who has been arrogant or superior in his dealings with Asians, or who has shown a low standard in his personal or public life. We in the West easily distinguish between convinced Christians, those whose allegiance is nominal, and those who make no Christian profession. But such a separation of religion and culture is completely strange to most peoples. The rejection of the Christian West because of the past history of imperialism, because of the assumption of racial superiority, because of wars and divisions, carries with it a general discrediting of the religion of the West—Christianity.

If the Christian community in Asia, small as it is, is to witness that "God so loved the *world*", not just the Christians or the West, then it must show itself as capable of growing in Asian soil. Indeed, the ideal of a self-governing, self-supporting, and self-propagating Church is almost a condition of existence. But not a self-sufficient Church. One of the tasks of the foreigner who is privileged to work to-day in a church in Asia is to help the Church to show forth the reality of the Christian community in contrast to the divisions of race and nation. The National Christian Council of India, in their statement to the Government justifying the continuance of missionaries in the country, take as their main argument the fact that the Church is supra-national. The presence in the service of the Church of those from other countries is necessary, they say, to demonstrate this fact about the nature of the Church. Any missionary who has worked in India, for example, since independence, can testify to the rare quality of friendship that Indians, Christians and others, are ready to offer a man or woman who is known to be without race consciousness, and who takes his or her place among Indian colleagues according to ability and not to status. Such a person has a tremendous opportunity to interpret (not necessarily to justify) the West to Asian minds and to help to overcome many misunderstandings.

These changes have brought new opportunities. They have allowed misunderstandings of the nature of the Church to be replaced by what is perhaps a truer conception. God in his wisdom and providence allowed the Church to be planted and to take root in these countries before the break with the West took place. The Church of India, Burma and Ceylon, the Batak Church, the Church of Christ in China, are not "foreign" churches. Foreign leadership and foreign money may be cut off, but Christ and His Church remain. Indeed, in Indonesia, where bitterness against Dutch political domination was turned also against the missionaries, a bad situation became the occasion for new discoveries in church relationships. The Dutch missionaries had to be asked, for the good of the church, to leave the country. Indonesian leadership developed rapidly and responsibly, but could never be sufficient for the total task in that tremendous archipelago. So the churches there requested help from abroad— from Switzerland, Australia, Germany, America, and also from Holland. A Dutchman who is "asked for" is very different from one who is "sent". By including Holland among the countries to which requests were sent they showed their intention that political division should not divide Christians. The Church of Christ is the place of forgiveness and reconciliation.

Apart from pride and joy in national independence, there is now a quite new consciousness of solidarity among Asian countries. In colonial days, all the lines went direct from the mother country to the dependency—Britain to India, U.S.A. to the Philippines, France to Indo-China, Holland to the Dutch East Indies. In reverse, the brightest scholars from these countries were sent to be trained in the universities of the "mother country". Trade and commercial links were established. There was little exploring of the different European cultures and very little contact between one Asian country and another.

Now that has largely changed. The Asian countries are discovering that in pre-colonial days (in some cases many centuries ago) there were cultural ties between one part of Asia and another. There was a time of Hindu expansion into Indonesia and Indo-China. The Buddhist faith spread from India right across Japan. These links are being taken up again—witness the Buddhist World Council meeting in Rangoon, and cultural missions to and from China. Equally, they are becoming aware that their economic problems are similar. Now that solutions have to be found in their own countries and not in London or Amsterdam or New York, they are eager to listen to and learn from each other. Asia, largely under leadership from India, has become aware of her political rôle between the Eastern and Western blocs. And the Afro-Asian Conference held in 1955 in Bandoeng shows that Asia is now prepared to play tutor to Africa and to give her all possible help and encouragement in her efforts towards political freedom.

While these countries have been coming into touch with each other politically and culturally, the Churches too have come together. Ever since 1949, when an East Asian Conference of Christian Leaders was held, Dr. Rajah Manikam of India has been travelling among the Asian countries as East Asian Secretary of the International Missionary Council and of the World Council of Churches. He has been telling them news of each other, interpreting events, making the churches conscious of the greatness of their task, and encouraging them to help one another.

One Conference on Literature and Literacy led to the formation of a centre from which Christian literature for Chinese speaking people could be prepared and distributed to Formosa, Hong Kong, Malaya, Indonesia and Thailand. Another Conference took up the themes for the Second Assembly of the World Council of Churches and studied them in the light of the Asian situation, leading to further plans for relating Christian work more closely to social and economic needs. A third came together on the subject of The Christian Home.

The churches in this part of the world have also discovered

that the missionary task of the Church is not a West-to-East affair, but is the task of the Church wherever it is; to the world, wherever the Gospel needs to be preached. And their answer to the "missionary follows the flag" theory is to go themselves where there is no flag to follow. So missionaries go from Indian churches to East Africa, to Indonesia and Papua, from the Philippines to Thailand, and a Philippino is directing the policy of an American Board of Missions in its work in South-East Asia.

The Christian answer to the tremendous change that has crept over the world scene cannot be summed up by Western missionary withdrawal and Asian solidarity. Perhaps the beginning of an answer is found when the churches of the world, and not only the nations of the world, begin to work together.

"The Nations are falling apart, but the Churches are drawing together", said the World Christian Youth Conference in 1939. And when Christians began to meet again after the 1939-45 War, it was found that they were not strangers to one another. As Bishop Berggrav of Norway said, the Churches knew each other better at the end than they did at the beginning, for they had tried to live and act and pray according to the will of God and not to be themselves the victims of war mentality.

So to-day, when everybody is organising internationally, the Churches, for all their national and denominational divisions, also have their world bodies, the International Missionary Council and the World Council of Churches. This is no pale imitation of a prevailing fashion. Christians have, in fact, through their missionary work and world movements, far more experience in internationalism than any political body. They are brought increasingly to think and act together on a world scale to show the world that the only true basis of unity is in turning to God who made heaven and earth, and who so loves the world that He sent His Son to save it.

II

"So You are a King?"

"Pilate said to him, 'So you are a king?' Jesus answered, 'You say that I am a king. For this cause I have come into the world, to bear witness to the Truth'." (John 18 : 37)

"The Church should keep out of politics," say many people. Yet it was finally the political charge that brought Jesus to the Cross. It was a trumped-up charge, in which neither the Jewish leaders nor Pilate believed. Only Jesus Himself acknowledged it as true!

The Jews brought forward the charge that Jesus was a political rebel and an enemy of Caesar, because only on such grounds could he be put to death. Pilate never acknowledged the charge. He did not, in fact, condemn Jesus, but "delivered him up to their will". (Luke 23:25). But in nailing over the Cross the superscription "Jesus of Nazareth, King of the Jews", in giving him at his death the title that had so alarmed Herod at his birth, Pilate acted more truly than he knew.

Jesus, fulfilling God's promise to his Chosen People, the Jews, was their King. Jesus, rejected by the Jews, became Head of the Church, the New Israel. And the Church, when it has been true to its Lord, has always been a political factor, and often a disturbing one in the life of society. For the very presence of the Church witnesses that there is a God in heaven to whom every knee in heaven and earth shall bow; that there is an "ultimate authority", and that man plays the rôle of omnipotence only at his peril.

WHEN China became a Communist country, many people in the West were greatly distressed that the same terms of abuse were used against missionaries as against Western Governments. They were "imperialist aggressors", "warmongers", "enemies of the people", and described in other such terms which are scarcely related in the Western mind to the normal activities of missionaries. "Surely", we said, "Christian missionary activity speaks for itself. It is clear for all to see that missionaries do not have their policy dictated by Government; that they are often critical of the Governments of the West; that they, above all Westerners, have cared for the ordinary people; schools, hospitals, and churches are there to testify to it." Yet not only did the official attack by Communists go on, but many Chinese Christians, some of whom had been close friends of the missionaries, joined in the accusations and set their names to them. Was this sheer lack of courage and conviction? Was it fear of their own standing and future, while the missionaries could go home, or what was it that led to these accusations which made so many missionaries feel that even those of their own household had turned against them?

One suggested explanation may be found, not in China, but in the Bible. In the New Testament one of the great disputes between John the Baptist and the Pharisees, between Jesus and the Pharisees, and between Paul and the Judaising party, was over the question of being "Children of Abraham". "We have Abraham as our father," say the Jews. "It is men of faith who are the sons of Abraham," says Paul. In other words, right through the Bible, right through history, runs the common assumption, challenged only by the tradition that led to Christianity, that race and religion go together. To be a Jew was to describe both race and religion, therefore Jews were conscientiously exempt from Emperor worship which was the Roman cult. To-day, when one crosses the frontier into Pakistan, the frontier guard fills in particulars of travellers in a big book where one of the columns is headed "religion". What he enters is not

Muslim, Hindu or Christian, but Pakistani, Indian or British. It is taken for granted that one's religion is the cultural expression of the nation to which one belongs. The Communist seeking political revolution attacks every religion because he understands religion or "ideology" as a kind of cultural cement. Remove the cement, and the building can easily be pulled down.

Therefore to a Chinese, a Westerner, be he representative of Government, trade, or religion, is expressing one thing only— his Western thought form (and the thought form of the West is Christianity). Even more, a Chinese Communist, schooled in Marxism, taught that all ideologies interpret a situation which is created by economic condition, would see in *any* emissaries of the West, whatever their ostensible purpose, the servants of the economic necessities of their country of origin. There is, according to the Marxist, no other way of accounting for human behaviour. Therefore, if the West must go, the missionary must go too.

Furthermore, they said, by not understanding this way in which human behaviour is determined, certain Chinese had unwittingly made themselves dupes of foreign powers. They had become Christians and thereby allied themselves with the imperialist West and committed themselves to carry out the will and further the economic interests of the foreigner. They had accepted money, which means that they were bribed. They had gone abroad for education, therefore they had been indoctrinated. What was true in their experience of the Soviet Union and of Communist doctrine was clearly equally operative in the West. Therefore any Chinese Christian who cared for his country, who believed as most do that the present régime has more possibilities in it than the former ones, is bound to prove to his fellows that he has severed all links with foreign powers, that he receives neither money nor correspondence, that he now understands the nature of the missionary involvement in the policies of the West, and that he denounces the lot. Religion has never been a thing to be fanatical about in China. No one will prevent him worshipping the way he likes, so long as he proves in all other ways that he has grasped and made his own the thought-world of the new China. This is to push the Christian faith back into the realm of a man's "private life", and to make it a matter of "private opinion" while all public policy is determined by national interest.

The big conflict over Christian participation in Shinto worship in Japan before the War had a similar basis. To perform cere-monies at the Shinto shrine was a mark of respect to the Japanese Emperor; it was not, they said, "religion". By this they probably meant that religion was a private affair—"what a man does", as Whitehead said, "with his solitariness", but to show respect to the Emperor is what binds the nation together. If this is not called "religion" it is because what goes by that name is of less importance in national life.

India is going through an intense struggle over the same question of religions and national unity. It was a conflict of religions which divided Pakistan from India, but while Pakistan is 90 per cent Muslim, India still has big religious minorities. How is the nation to become one?

India decided to become a "secular" state. This means that the Government seeks to care for the good of the community as a whole, without reference to the religious allegiance of its citizens. It allows freedom to its citizens to profess, practise and propagate their own religion, without interference or disability from the state. But this view of "secular Government" grew up in the West, continuing a long history in which Roman and Jewish ideas of righteousness, justice, impartiality, had been baptised into Christianity and become the accepted background of whole nations, whether the individuals were consciously Christian or not.

It has been taken over in India by those who had their whole political education and training under the British. Pandit Nehru, who is an agnostic, describes himself as having had a "Muslim environment, a Hindu upbringing, and a Christian outlook." He has absorbed all the best traditions of integrity, justice, tolerance, of the West, and interpreted them in a non-Christian environment. The Vice-President, Dr. Radhakrishnan, held a Chair in Philosophy in Oxford and is a great example of "Philosopher-politician". He is the most learned and attractive exponent of a liberalised Hinduism. The President, Dr. Prasad, is a practising orthodox Hindu, yet also trained in the British tradition of disinterested public service. What happens when these men give way to others? Here is the way that a young Indian Christian college lecturer tries to explain the Indian situation to her fellow Christians:—

"To the Hindu through the ages religion has been more real than political power. He naturally believes that religion means the same to others. Let us remember that his nation and religion are one and the same thing. . . . India has been a nation for centuries . . . we know that in the *political* sense of the word she was not one . . . yet in ancient days the link of religion was forged which welded the diverse elements of race and custom together. Thus it was that Hindu and Indian gradually became synonymous terms. The Hindu does not have any extra-territorial ties. He can only look upon international relations, such as in the United Nations, from a political angle, and as a matter of expediency. But he can never comprehend the Muslim, Christian, or Buddhist idea of Brotherhood across national borders. He can never comprehend it, for he has never experienced it. In fact, any extra-territorial tie for him means taking away from one hundred per cent national loyalty."[1]

India, then, is likely before long to be facing a powerful struggle to establish Hinduism as the "national religion".

This desire for a national religion is already evident in Ceylon. Ceylon is rejoicing in her own government after having been ruled successively by the Portuguese (with a Roman Catholic culture), the Dutch (who brought the Reformed Faith), and the

[1] *The Fear of the Minority;* N.C.C. Review, India. August 1954.

British (with the Church of England as their Established Church). Now the people of Ceylon have their own government, and, following custom, tend to "establish" Buddhism as the official religion of the country. Where before there were Anglican chaplaincies, there are now Buddhist priests. Buddhist symbols are used for decoration on State occasions, and Government sponsorship is given to the celebration of great occasions in Buddhist history.

What is the place of the Christian Churches in these countries? Rarely do they form more than 2 per cent of the population. In "colonial" days, however little support the Government gave to missionaries, the Christian groups inevitably gained a certain amount of protection and moral support from being of the same faith as the ruling power. On the other hand, they suffered from being suspect as "pro-foreigner". They were often regarded as politically unreliable in the struggle for independence. Now the foreign support has gone and the suspicion remains. Is there any place for them in a country which is trying to weld itself into unity? Is religion a matter of private opinion, in which case the Christians might keep quietly on with their own form of worship, neither disturbing nor disturbed—or is it an expression of national life, and if so, should they conform and adopt the national religion?

Jesus went to the Cross as a protest against these two ideas of religion as a national ideology or a private belief. And his death was the culmination of a struggle that began when God called Abraham and chose him to be the bearer of the true knowledge of God "that in him all the peoples of the world might be blest". That promise is being fulfilled to-day in these little minority groups, planted in almost every country of the world to witness that there is a God in heaven and that Jesus claims Kingship over our individual hearts certainly, but equally over our national and community life.

The Conference of Christian leaders from East Asian countries expressed this forcefully in these words: "The gospel proclaims that God's sovereignty includes all realms of life. Christ sitting at the right hand of God reigns, and the Church owes it to the world to remind it constantly that it lives under his judgment and grace. . . . Only the knowledge of the ultimate accountability of man and society to God, and of the grace of God by which men, being forgiven, forgive one another, can be the foundation of personal responsibility and responsible society. The lack of the knowledge of God as the Judge of history is at the root of all tendencies towards nihilism and totalitarianism in Asia and elsewhere".[1]

In the Soviet Union, the continued existence of the Church under Communist rule has disproved Marxist theory that the Church will disintegrate, but not discouraged Marxists in their efforts to wear it away. In some of the European countries where Christian communities have centuries of political experience behind them the voice of the Church can be heard, declaring the Judgment and the Mercy of God. But can we expect the same of the churches of Africa and Asia?

The foreign missionary movement was at its height at the time when Christian thought was concentrated far more on individual salvation than on corporate life in any form. The Christian Gospel had its social consequences in the changed life of the communities that became Christian, and in concern for the outcasts and underprivileged in all societies, but it is only in the last twenty years or so that the older churches have been reawakened to think of themselves as the watchmen of God in the life of their nations. How much less have "new" Christians in the younger churches been prepared and taught and trained for such a task!

In India new resources of national leadership are being found in the ancient Christian community of Malabar. Many of this community, finding no "social relevance" in their traditional

[1] The Christian Prospect in Eastern Asia, I.M.C., pp. 114-5.

26

faith, have abandoned it in practice and become Communists. Others, stimulated by contact with Western Christian social thinking, are joining with those from more recently established churches in giving a lead both to the nation and to the Christians by interpreting public questions in Christian terms. The National Christian Council, representing the great majority of Protestant Christians, can assure the Government in a public statement that "there can be no doubt about the Church's responsibility to adhere loyally to the purpose of the Government in maintaining law and order, and in the provision of the welfare of all people in the nation. The Church supports the Government in every way consistent with the interests of justice. It does this not as a matter of expediency, but because a concern for human welfare and justice is a fundamental result of the 'love for neighbour' instilled by Jesus Christ".[1]

This is not "my country, right or wrong", but Paul's injunction "Fear God, honour the King"—in other words "Support and encourage in Christian obedience what is for the common welfare, but be ready at all times to resist a Government which acts in the interests of only a section of the community, which permits injustice, or which takes to itself absolute power."

Indonesia is another country where the churches are trying to think politically. They felt a great sense of responsibility at the time when the new Constitution was being worked out, to establish a State which would not only grant religious freedom but would be positively just and responsible in all its dealings. Dr. Leimena, a Christian leader who has held office in every Cabinet since independence, constantly urges that Christians must be both good Christians and good Indonesians—seeking the good of the whole community.

A recent statement issued by the Christian Council in Nigeria shows that they too are eager that self-government shall be good government. As Christians and as citizens, Christians are urged

[1] N.C.C. Review, May 1955, p. 202.

to exercise their right to vote, for "it is the will of God that the country should enjoy good government, that is, that it should have a government which promotes the physical and moral welfare of the people by efficient planning and administration, makes justice available for all, secures freedom and rights of conscience of minorities."

They make a further point that good government requires men and women of ability and integrity in administration: "Every Christian should set an example to others by his truthfulness, honesty and kindliness, both in the elementary duties of citizenship and in the more responsible offices of the State. Christians are called to recognise that they hold their possessions, talents and any authority given to them by the civil community as stewards, who in the end are accountable to God. . . . Bribery and corruption should be banished by the vigilance of the authorities, the faithful witness of the Church, and the absolute refusal of all citizens to take or offer bribes."[1]

The statement closes with the sober comment: "It needs always to be remembered that the voice of the people is not always the voice of God, and that good government can never of itself produce the Kingdom of God on earth."

Would that this sense of corporate responsibility could be taken for granted, East or West; but the view of Christianity as concerned only with personal salvation still holds sway. A description of the Revival Movement in Kenya, which has put up such magnificent resistance to Mau Mau and brought new light to many darkened and frustrated souls, ends with words which would be equally applicable in many other parts of the world: "The kind of problem, political, economic, social, which is at present exercising the mind of the Kikuyu, is not one to which the majority of keen Christians in the country is seriously directing its attention. To many Kikuyu, the Christian message seems irrelevant to the burning issues of the hour."

[1] Reported E.P.S. No. 27, 1955.

28

This is part of the Cross that the Church must carry today, the dilemma of "How could it have been otherwise?" facing the knowledge that we have not done all we should to make known to the nations that they are answerable to God as Lord and Judge for their dealings with His children.

One way in which the churches and missionary bodies together are attempting to do this is through the Churches' Commission on International Affairs. Through this body, set up in 1948 by the joint action of the International Missionary Council and the World Council of Churches, the churches have a means of speaking with one voice to the new international organisations which play such a big part in the present day.

If it is urgent that the witness of the church should be heard in the policies of the nations, it is no less urgent to speak to these international bodies: the United Nations, UNESCO, the International Labour Office, and many others.

The Churches' Commission on International Affairs sees its task not primarily as looking after Christian or ecclesiastical interests but as bringing to bear the best informed minds of the churches wherever decisions affecting human destinies are being made.

The refugee problem is a clear example of this. Again and again, whenever there has been a tendency to "shelve" the refugee problem, or to close down international help before the last refugee was settled, C.C.I.A. has been able to bring before the responsible agency the urgency of continuing action, in ways which did not damage or ignore human personality and dignity, and which were commensurate with the need. And C.C.I.A. was able to do this because, through the World Council Service to Refugees, the churches were deeply committed to active work among the refugees themselves.

In another way, the great services of intercession which have been held in Geneva at the time of important international meetings as well as in other centres at other similar times, have been occasions to speak directly to those in whose hands great decisions lay. One example of this is the sermon preached by the Bishop of Chichester at the opening of the Conference on the Peaceful Uses of Atomic Energy. Taking as his text, "I have set before you life and death, blessing and cursing: therefore choose life, that both thou and thy seed may live" (Deut. 30: 19), he spoke of the discovery of the secret of atomic energy as unlocking the gate into a new world and stressed the consequences of the decision that had been made to use atomic power for destruction: "To let hell loose on earth before anyone else can do so, or to inflict certain destruction on others as a way of preventing possible injury to ourselves is to break God's commandments. But to develop atomic energy for peaceful uses, not only for ourselves but for those in greater need, is to be a fellow-worker with God."[1]

The resolutions on Disarmament brought by C.C.I.A. to the Central Committee of the World Council of Churches at Davos, 1955, show that the churches are not always in the position of rubber-stamping decisions of secular bodies, but are prepared to make suggestions on their own account:—

"Two tasks appear especially urgent:
(1) to devise a system of inspection and control;
(2) to find a starting point for the reduction of armaments.
. . . Since there is so much uncertainty as to what is scientifically necessary for reliable inspection and control, we suggest that the United Nations establish an international commission of scientists and technicians to identify the essential scientific requirements for an adequate system. . . ."[2]

They further list six steps which might be taken to bring any critical international situation under control. These are suggestions made in the hope of stimulating governments to develop and utilise methods for the peaceful settlement of disputes.[3] It

[1] Ecumenical Review, October 1955, p. 1.
[2] Ecumenical Review, October 1955, p. 67.
[3] E.P.S. No. 32, 1955.

was, in fact, thanks to a proposal from C.C.I.A. that Peace Observation Teams were set up by the U.N., one of which helped greatly in aiding the restoration of peaceful post-war relations in the Balkans.

C.C.I.A. is not only acting *for* the churches. It is also helping them to learn how to act. So often, says the Director, on questions not affecting the churches directly, but concerning human welfare and right relations, no word can be said because the churches take only a limited view of their responsibility. They have not got the "set up" or the people of experience in international affairs who can express, train or test Christian opinion. The churches acting together cannot do what the churches frequently do not know how to do in their own sphere. So the churches are learning out of the necessity of the hour that they cannot stand back and look on as decisions are taken and history is made. They stand not only at the bar of history, but before the Judgment seat of God, to answer for what happens in the world.

III

"Are You the Son of God?"

"And they all said, 'Are you the Son of God then?' And He said
to them, 'You say that I am'." (Luke 22 : 70)

*The Jewish religious leaders began plotting against Jesus as
soon as they realised the claims that he was making. He broke in
on their religious system, for to accept his claim would be to
bring Jewish ritual—all focussed on the coming Messiah—to an
end. The natural reaction of any established system to Jesus is
"Away with Him. Give us Barabbas, Barabbas is one of us. We
can understand violence and wrong doing. It is within our
experience. But Jesus disturbs us. We don't like his criticism of
our religious leaders, his 'knowing better' than our teachers. We
had life under control. Now questions begin to arise, so let us
put an end to uncertainty by getting rid of him. Then we can
continue to serve God as we know how."*

*A few among the leaders (we can think of Nicodemus and
Joseph of Arimathea) were prepared to listen to him, but for the
rest it was only a case of waiting to find the occasion and the
charge to have him put out of the way, so that religious life
could go on undisturbed.*

*Jesus' claim to be not only the Messiah of the Jews but the
definitive revelation of God is challenged and resisted by every
religion and philosophy. Yet he came not to destroy but to fulfil
the promises of God to the Jewish people. Those of any race or
religion who accept him become heirs of the Promise also.*

WE said at the beginning of the last chapter that the question of the children of Abraham was one of the great points of dispute between Jesus and his opponents in the Gospels. We have looked at the case of those who identify religion and culture or who see in religion the force which binds them together as a nation. Why do we have to challenge this? Is it not a fact, and an important one to be reckoned with in any political dealings with another people? One of the fundamental principles of the British in the days of imperialism was that native custom should be disturbed as little as possible. The East India Company in India set its face against anything that would "disturb the native". When the British accepted the invitation of the Sultans in Malaya to administer the country, it was on the understanding, still respected, that the religion of the rulers would not be interfered with.

Other people would object on other grounds to any attempt to persuade people to change their religion. "Do not all roads lead to God?" is the frequent question of the Hindu. "As those who follow different roads up a mountain find themselves together at the top, so all seekers after God will arrive at the summit where God is. God is too great to be defined. Let us each go our own way in search of Him." Such humility and apparent tolerance before the greatness of divine truth is immensely attractive to many Christians. It seems to give common ground to those who believe in God over against secularists and materialists and especially Communists. "Should not all who believe in spiritual values make common cause?" In fact, many are doing so. When the United Nations held its tenth anniversary celebrations at San Francisco early in 1955, the San Francisco Council of Churches invited representatives of the world's religions to a Festival of Faith at which prayers were offered by Jews, Muslims, Buddhists, Bahaists, Hindus, and Christians. (Roman Catholics did not co-operate). The report says: "It made clear at the beginning of the U.N. meeting that *religious people of the world* want peace."[1]

[1] Christianity and Crisis, July 25th, 1955 (author's italics).

c

But the Christian answer to those who don't want to disturb people's patterns of life is that this is exactly what Christ came to do, and exactly what God had been doing from the time he so disturbed Abraham that he left the culture of Ur of the Chaldees and set off on a journey. God breaks in on human life saying "No" to every system of natural religion. That is how he became known as "a jealous God". He called men out from identifying religion with race or nation, so that one inherited one's religion by natural descent, or identifying it with the land, so that there were "territorial gods". By the Covenant relationship which he established with Abraham, with Israel on Mount Sinai, and then with the Church through the death of Christ, he denied the assertion of the mystics that he is only to be known by withdrawal from the world, and showed that it is God, not man, who crosses the gulf that separates man from God. Christians are often accused, especially in India, of being intolerant. In the sense that they cannot accept that all religions should live side by side on equal terms, they must be.

But this does not mean any lack of understanding or sympathy for those of other religions. Rather it means that we believe, with St. Paul, that in Christ God has made known for all men the clue to the mystery of life which all religions are seeking to answer. Every religion is an answer to the questions which are in every man's heart: "Why was I born? Where do I come from? Where do I go? What is life for? Why must I suffer?" To all this Paul answers in his magnificent opening to the Epistle to the Ephesians: "He has made known to us the mystery of his will." All our questions about the purpose or meaning of life, whether we be Hindu or Muslim, Jew, Bahai or animist, are answered in Christ.

When Paul stood in the market place in Ephesus or Corinth or Rome, he came as one whose own pattern of life had been broken by Jesus on the Damascus road, but also gloriously re-fashioned. He knew "the glory that was Greece" and "the greatness that was Rome". He was immensely proud to be a Roman citizen. But, he said, something had happened which threw a completely new light on everything, including the Roman Empire. More important than to be a Roman citizen, which could be achieved by birth or by buying oneself in, was to be a citizen of God's kingdom—and the way into that kingdom had just been opened for everyone by this Roman crucifixion in Jerusalem. It was important, it was news, and it was urgent.

When Carey went to India, against the will of the East India Company, against the judgment of the church people in his own country, he was aware that India was a deeply religious country. It had its own answers to the questions "Who?" and "Why?" and "Where?" Hinduism started from the universal experience of suffering and explained it by the wheel of existence—what one was in this life was determined by what one had been in a previous existence. What one would be was determined by what one was in this life. There was no escape except to accept one's fate and to try to set a distance between oneself and the illusory reality of the world. By becoming increasingly spiritual one might, as it were, disembody oneself and be released from the endless circle of rebirth into the nothingness of no-suffering. To this Carey said "No! There is another key to unlock the mystery of existence. It is not described by a wheel but a Cross. God knows our suffering. He came himself to share it and to break the closed circle. The answer is not 'nothingness' but life with God—here and hereafter."

Judson went into Burma, to a country which, apart from the hill-tribes, had wholly adopted a religion which had been swept out of India because it attempted to reform Hinduism. Buddha, like the Hindu seers, was deeply conscious of the problem of suffering—even the suffering he caused to minute insects when he put his foot to the ground. Yet the illumination which came to him was not that one should abstract oneself from suffering but rather that through compassion and service, through ridding oneself of desire, which is at the root of all suffering, one should win through to peace. "So to live that when death comes it may not find me hankering for life."[1]

To such as these Adoniram Judson and those who followed had to say: "Salvation from suffering is not something that by self-discipline and compassion you may attain for yourself. You are too closely involved in the world ever to free yourself from it by your own effort. Yet the good news is that God has done this for you and all men in the life and death and resurrection of Jesus Christ. We tell you of the free gift of life which is yours here and hereafter in Jesus Christ."

A Christian minister, a convert from Hinduism, elected to stay in Pakistan at the time of partition rather than join his people in India. He preached in the open streets of a Muslim town and was mobbed by young Muslims, struck in the face and held prisoner for most of a night. The Muslims have their own way of dealing with the problems of life. It has been a faith which "asks no questions and gives no answers", but it prescribes a way of life, in which to walk is the way of security, it provides a fellowship and brotherhood, which to forsake is treason to be punished by death, and it has "indelibly ingrained in its system the conviction that the world's rightful destiny is to become the domain of the Islamic Empire".[2] To proclaim Christ crucified to the Muslim is perhaps the hardest task in the world, because he starts with a distorted view of Christianity, picked up by Mohamet himself from his contact with the 7th century churches. Yet a Christian minister is prepared to protest with his life against this, saying, "The picture of Christ which you present and reject is distorted, but the thought of God which you present and accept is distorted too. The unbridgable gap between God and man *has* been bridged. The Cross is, as it were, the ladder set up between earth and heaven. Life is not in terms of

[1] D. T. Niles, *Eternal Life—Now*. Footnote p. 27.

[2] J. W. Sweetman, *The Bible in Islam*, British & Foreign Bible Society.

obedience to a book, but obedience to a living Lord, who became Man and dwelt among us, and who sits at God's right hand. He it is who creates fellowship within His Church, and the destiny of the world is to become his Kingdom."

A missionary goes to live among primitive peoples in the mountains of Formosa or the forests of Africa—people whose lives are often dominated by the idea of spirits who show their anger by causing illness or bad harvests or drought, who must be placated and who never leave one alone. People sometimes talk as though to bring them the knowledge of the Cross of Christ were to upset the simplicity of faith in favour of something abstract and difficult to believe. It was a Chinese who had himself known the power of spirit worship who said, "You have no idea of the immense simplification of life which the Gospel brings." For such people too the Cross is like the key to a puzzle. Set it at the centre and life becomes meaningful and orderly. One is no longer at the mercy of wilful spirits with their unpredictable whims, but in the safe hands of a God made known in Jesus Christ whose purpose for all men is love.

A group of young people of many nations and churches went in 1953 to an industrial town in Sweden, where an atheist Town Council has for twenty years refused permission for a church to be built; they set up a bell tower and dug the foundations for a church. They knew that Sweden has all the material wealth to satisfy the needs of its citizens. It is equalitarian and peaceful. It has not been involved in wars or in imperialism. Yet to set up a church is to say "No" to a society which answers men's questions in terms of material satisfaction and prosperity. It is to set up in the midst of a satisfied society a reminder of the suffering of others, a reminder that this world is not the whole story but that one stands before the mercy and judgment of God—answerable for the use one makes of the material world in which one is set.

And when even school children in East Germany resist the pressure to make them give up their church youth groups, when they are prepared to sacrifice the chance of higher education and often to bring their families into trouble, they too are saying "No" to a view of life which says, "You only exist and have significance as you consciously take part in the inevitable working out of economic change which will lead to the ideal proletarian society." They can say "No", even though as school children they may not have all the answers at their finger tips, because their badge is the Cross over the World: the sign that the world is not controlled by inevitable forces within itself, but is in the hands of God, who has claimed it for Himself by the death of Christ on the Cross. We are not caught on the moving band of inevitable progression, but we are the children of God, made for fellowship with him and with one another: a "status" which is not ours by right of our nation or class or even our human nature, but which has been won for us by Christ on the Cross.

To protest and resist is always easier than to affirm and construct. Yet the churches which have sought to proclaim the Gospel by personal evangelism have tried at the same time to show the consequences of Christian belief in concrete and convincing form. They have tried to make available for others by education the knowledge they were seeking to convey. They have tried to proclaim Christ as the Lord of Life by showing their regard for life in medical service. They have tried, though to a lesser extent, to break the sense of fatalism and show the goodness of God in improved methods of agriculture, hygiene, diet, and community life. And they have established churches. All these activities had the one purpose of showing forth the glory of "Him who brought us out of darkness into His glorious light."

Education

Here again the Church has to bear the burden of suffering in seeing the gifts accepted but so often without regard to the Giver. "We are grateful to the missionaries for coming to bring us education," said an African student in London some years ago. "We are thankful that it was Christian education. Now we must have these benefits for all our people, not just for as many as you can send missionaries to teach. Christian education if possible, but in any case education."

In country after country where education has been introduced by Christian missions, education is now, rightly, becoming a Government responsibility and universal education is the aim. In parts of Africa missions continue to staff their own schools but receive grants from the Government. Where education is rapidly expanding, it is clear that it would be short-sighted to limit Christian influence to mission-controlled schools, and so the policy is increasingly to concentrate on teacher-training, hoping in this way to pass on to the education service generally a constant supply of Christian teachers, who have trained in a Christian institution.

In South Africa great distress has been caused by the Bantu Education Act. This Act makes it a condition of receiving Government subsidies that schools should conform to the official policy, based on the view that education for the Bantu differs radically in purpose and scope from that given to Europeans. The missions, conscientiously unable to accept this distinction, found themselves forced to hand over their schools completely, or to continue them with privately raised funds. This latter has clearly only been possible in certain cases, and there has been general agreement between missions as to which schools should be privately maintained and which handed over. In some cases, it is hoped to continue contact with former Christian schools through hostels and chaplains. This victory for the theory of separate development of black and white is looked on with dismay.

The churches in India also have found themselves faced by serious and difficult decisions. There has for many years been a growing conviction in both Christian and non-Christian circles that education, as it was developed under the British *raj*, was

39

too little adapted to the needs of the predominantly rural population. "There is no use", says Bishop Newbigin in a circular letter of October 1955, "expanding an education which is merely going to ruin the villages and flood the towns with unemployed youth." But a hopeful line of development has been found on the basis of the ideas introduced by Gandhi and known as Basic Education. This "aims to bring the child into a small community in which each shall have his part to play, and in which children are taught to live simply and as far as possible to supply their own needs. . . . Learning is correlated with a basic craft such as spinning, weaving or agriculture." But this has become not merely a system of education but training for a way of life, which reflects Gandhi's own views about the place of worship in a community. Bishop Newbigin writes of the tension and searching of conscience that this has caused among Christians who are otherwise anxious to share in what they believe to be a forward step in Indian elementary education: —

"The aim is to build up loyalty to a community which transcends religious loyalties which are felt to be sectional and divisive. This creates a severe conflict of loyalties for Christians. Some sincere Christians believe that they can play their part in the service of the nation by taking part in this sort of worship. The vast majority feel it to be impossible. . . . The C.S.I. has put forth an official statement advising Christian students in Basic Schools that they cannot take part in the 'common worship', and also suggesting positive ways in which they can make their contribution to the life of the school."

He goes on to show that in this issue the Church may be coming near a real meeting with Hinduism: —

"Caste, idolatry, polytheism, evil social customs of all kinds —these were things rightly to be criticised. Hardly any Hindus now defend them seriously. But to-day we are being brought right up against the central question: Is there a way of reconciliation with God, and therefore of mutual reconciliation among men, apart from Jesus Christ? And that question is posed, not in an academic way, but in the practical daily decisions which have to be taken by ordinary citizens and ordinary students in Basic Schools."

This raises very sharply the further question which is pressing for an answer in all parts of the world: What is Christian education? Bible knowledge (in which many Hindus excel)? Character training? Secular education opened by school prayers? Or opening up for the growing young person the wonder of God's all-embracing purpose for the world?

West African Governments send over to Britain every year for advanced training men and women who are going to fill key posts in the rapidly expanding educational system. Almost without exception they have been through Christian schools and many are themselves Christians. They begin in this country by going to Church. But the churches are half-empty, the atmosphere is cold. They see how small a part church-going plays here. They remember the colonial servants whose places they are to fill, who were rarely in church except on formal occasions. They are deeply concerned that self-government in their territories should be good government. They know that that is not only a question of laws but of the people who administer them. But they think they know better now than to see any connection between the church, education, and training for life in a new nation. Among the most important evangelistic work which is being done these days is by University lecturers, overseas student chaplains and others, who sit down with groups such as these African educationists and think through with them in the light of the Christian understanding of life, their tasks in training the first generation to grow up in a self-governing West Africa.

Health

"Health and wholeness" is a great part of the meaning of salvation. One of the clearest signs that the Messiah had come was that "the blind receive their sight, and the lame walk, the lepers are cleansed, and the deaf hear" (Matt. 11 : 5). Strangely, to our ears, Jesus followed this account of his own mission with the words, "And blessed is he, who shall find no occasion of stumbling in me." Here was the visible evidence that God was at work restoring his creation, fighting against the forces that destroy. But the evidence was not enough. The opponents of Jesus kept asking for "signs", for indisputable proofs. Not getting what they wanted, they accused Jesus of blasphemy.

In Arabia, a Muslim country, and Nepal, a Buddhist one, the only entry for a Christian missionary is, up till now, through medical work. Time and again the healing skill and compassion of doctor and nurse have opened a way for the story of the Great Physician to be told and heard. Recently, when a missionary doctor went into Arabia at the invitation of an Arab ruler, he explained that his main desire was to bring the people to a knowledge of Jesus Christ. The Arab ruler said, "You may try." So sure was he of the impenetrability of the Muslim faith that, for the sake of modern medicine, he would even receive it at the hands of a Christian. "We want medicine, at Christian hands if necessary, but in any case, medicine." "And Jesus, having compassion on the multitude, healed them all."

The medical missionary, or the doctor in a Christian hospital, longs and prays that men and women will see behind the healing the Great Healer, beyond the doctor and nurse fighting against disease, the power of God, made visible in the Cross, seeking to bring all things to perfection. But heal he must, whether people understand his greater purpose or not.

Frequently it has been Christian medical work which has forced on missionaries the necessity to try to change the conditions in which people live, otherwise the hospital becomes a "patching-up" station, but cannot raise the level of health. Hunger and wrong feeding inevitably weaken resistance. Use of the land so that soil-erosion sets in inevitably reduces fertility. Poor stock minimises food value and market price. Here and there missionaries with enthusiasm and experience in agriculture or village industries or community projects have tried to do something, but the task is too great to be mastered by local effort. The Technical School, and Agricultural Institute, started by missions, have been training men and women to give a lead to others. Now the international organisations have entered the field: W.H.O., F.A.O., UNICEF, and others.

This sharing of up-to-date methods is normally looked on as a purely humanitarian and technical process, raising no religious issues. Yet here, too, the Christian gospel is a key to a way of understanding man's relation to the physical world entirely different from that of other religions.

Technical Progress

"It is the will of Allah," says the Muslim. His acceptance of fate cuts at the root of all initiative or faith in the power to prevent disease or change conditions. So also with the Hindu. "In Calcutta", someone said, "are some of the best brains and the worst conditions in the world. Yet the brains will not apply themselves to changing the conditions." People are as they are —in city slums or famine-stricken villages—because that is where the wheel of fate has brought them.

There may be many origins of the scientific outlook of the West, Greek and Roman as well as Christian, and much of scientific discovery has so fascinated people that they act like men in the Old Testament and say, "*My* power and the might of *my* hand hath gotten me this wealth" (Deut. 8: 17). But back of the scientific outlook is the confidence expressed in the Genesis stories that God has given man dominion over the earth. It is his, under God, to subdue and cultivate. Those from the West who have so far forgotten their Christian origins that they take modern science as self-evident are leading those of other religions into dangerous places. Here too is a field for evangelism, for making clear the "open secret" of God's will and purpose.

It may be that the Church's work here must begin with the "technical experts". Whether or not they see the relevance of the Christian understanding for themselves, they may be able to see that, for those of other traditions, if one "world-view" is disturbed and destroyed it must be replaced by another, more adequate and more all-embracing.

Training and orientation like that which is being given in Britain by Oversea Service[1] may be of tremendous value. Once or twice every month for a brief six days, a group of people are brought together who are going abroad as Government servants, firms' representatives or on technical missions. Under Christian leadership they are helped to see the significance and consequence which both they and their jobs represent. They are helped to understand the "temper" of the country to which they go, the stage of its economic, social, and political development, the nature of its religious outlook. They are told of the Christian Church in that area, and shown how their personal lives, their leisure time activities, and the way they understand and interpret their work, can help or hinder the cause of Christ. It is hoped that in their new sphere of work they will act as responsible laymen of the Christian Church.

Church and Institution

Where, in all this, does the "indigenous" Church come in? One of the most difficult problems in passing over responsibility and leadership to the church-on-the-spot by the missionary bodies has been the relation of church and institution. The institutions, hospitals, schools, colleges, were established on Western lines in the faith that before the impact of Christian teaching and healing, the old religions would give way and there would be a great influx into the Christian Church. In fact, as we have seen, this did not happen. Instead of crumbling away, the old religions adapted themselves, borrowing from Christianity in such a way

[1] Edinburgh House, 2 Eaton Gate, London, S.W.1.

that it was possible to accept the benefits of Christian education and medicine without committing oneself to Christian belief. The Christian institutions also adapted themselves, being convinced that their freedom to proclaim the Gospel and, in the educational institutions, to have an influence on the lives of those who would be the leaders of their country, was worth while, even though they gained few converts. Alongside these centres of Christian service and influence a church grew up recruited on the whole from the humbler ranks of society. This has created a totally unbalanced situation. Economically, a church, poor in material resources, finds itself faced with responsibility for institutions far beyond its possibility to support or maintain. The solution sometimes proposed, to leave the institutions in the hands of the overseas missionary societies, while the indigenous church takes over the pastoral and evangelistic work, leads directly to a distorted view of the Church. It gives the impression that the Church's concern is with men's souls, and it can leave to others the life of the mind and body. But even worse, it gives the impression that the Westerners, who provide the money, judge the schools and hospitals as of more importance than the Church, since it is on these that they spend money and for these that they provide highly trained Western staff.

This disproportion is enhanced in the different professional standards which exist in the churches and in the institutions. While only men with recognised qualifications can hold posts in school or hospital, the graduate ministry in the Church is a very small proportion of the whole, while the great majority of pastors, however great their spiritual qualities and their devotion, have only limited scholarship. This again puts the Church at a disadvantage in relation to the student population. In West Africa, for example, children attending one of the magnificent modern-style schools under Western leadership, and receiving all their Christian education there, must find a great contrast in returning to the village church. The temptation to "floor" the pastor with awkward questions must be irresistible—and then it is easy to dismiss the Church as "behind the times".

This is one of the painful points of transition from "Missionary" to "Church" responsibility. It will not be resolved easily or quickly. Perhaps a West African leader gave a clue when he said, speaking about the influence of the Evanston Assembly on the Gold Coast: "We began to see that the church is not the end-product of evangelism, but the place where it begins. Too often the churches have been held up as exhibits of what the missionary effort has resulted in, rather than the starting places for the evangelism of our own people." As the churches themselves take up the task, they will decide for themselves how the three-fold ministry of Jesus—preaching, teaching and healing—is to be expressed.

IV

"He Saved Others"

"Those who passed by derided him, wagging their heads and saying 'You who would destroy the temple and build it in three days, save yourself!' So also the chief priests, with the scribes and elders mocked him, saying, 'He saved others, he cannot save himself. He is the King of Israel; let him come down now from the cross and we will believe in him; for he said, "I am the Son of God" '." (Matt. 27: 39-43)

It is not a pleasant picture of human nature that is given here. The leaders of the people had achieved their object. They had so managed to influence the populace that they got them to call for the release of Barabbas rather than Jesus. They had so intimidated Pilate that he handed Jesus over to their will. They might at least have let him die in peace. But they had to walk up and down in front of the Cross, gloating over their success and calling out taunts to add to the agony of Jesus. But, uncannily, their taunts, as their accusations, have become the Church's confession of faith: "Son of God, King of the Jews, he saved others, himself he cannot save."

All through the ministry of Jesus, the Pharisees had demanded a sign, "proof positive", that Jesus was the Messiah. They wanted a wonder worker who would disturb the order of creation, not a true representative of God who "was restoring all things to perfection". They could not see that there was nothing to add to his evidence of Messiahship in his teaching, preaching and healing except this, that he accepted even his death—and death on a cross—as part of his ministry of seeking and saving that which was lost.

47

Has the Church learnt this lesson of trusting itself utterly into the hands of God for life and death—of being unconcerned about its own public standing, so long as it is fulfilling its mission?

TO those who object to Christian missions on the ground that they are "disturbing a pattern of life" there is a further answer than that of the last chapter. We from the West have already radically disturbed the established patterns of the East and of Africa. It is not possible to govern a country, to trade with it, to introduce Western style education and medicine, to involve its men in Western warfare and to leave the life of its people untouched. Traders, travellers and conquerors have brought their own version of Western civilisation. When missionaries have followed, it has not always been as "running dogs" or "puppets". One of the incentives which took Dr. Schweitzer to Lambarene was, on the contrary, the desire in some way to atone for the harm done by traders who had exploited the African and introduced him to Western civilisation at its worst.

The impact of the West does not need to be at its worst to be disruptive. A young Christian leader from Burma who knows the whole of South-East Asia writes:—

"Asia has been exposed to the vigorous impact of the dynamic Western world with its technological emphasis, and its whole concept of life and its political and social structures have been thoroughly disturbed. . . . The outstanding obvious changes in the sphere of politics are but symbols and consequences of the general shift that is taking place. For . . . there are evidences of the revolution in other spheres of life—in the changing climate of thought, the ferment of ideas, the reassessment of economics and the new relationships in society."[1]

From Kenya someone describes the Mau Mau movement as "the sudden panic and complete internal collapse of a comparatively advanced tribe under the terrific strain of the impact of the white man over the last fifty years".

[1] Student World III '52. Some Trends in Changing Asian Society.

48

In Liberia, in an area up-country so mountainous that wheeled traffic has never been introduced, preparations are being made by scientists for mining by nuclear ray. No wonder that a speaker, trying to make vivid to his audience in Britain the rapidity of change, said: "It is as if one of you were to say, 'My aunt knew Boadicea'."

Not only has change been introduced by foreigners. Fijians are among the British forces in action in Malaya. Thousands of tribesmen from Africa as well as other British territories were enlisted in the Second World War. They left villages where every activity of social and agricultural life was controlled by custom and ritual and learnt the totally other discipline of modern warfare. They saw other countries and customs. They learnt mechanical skills. They may return to the same village but never to the old life, for the stronghold of the ancient gods has been destroyed.

If we believe that the "scientific outlook" has any even remote connection with God's instruction to man to "replenish the earth and subdue it"; if we believe that Western forms of government or education or medicine owe anything to the Christian understanding of life, then we are morally bound both to share these good things which have been entrusted to us for the benefit of all men, and to share all we know of God, to whom we and all men are answerable for the use we make of his gifts. We do not have the field to ourselves, nor is it left empty if we do not enter it. Human greed and selfishness are ready to make use of any new opportunity to serve their own purposes. The Communist interpretation is eagerly and promptly advanced in every situation of change, or the desert sand of secularism seeps in to destroy the life of the spirit.

"The peoples of Asia, Africa and Latin America are in ferment," says a recent statement from the World Council of Churches. "They have been awakened to a new sense of human dignity. They are in revolt against political and social conditions

49

that deny human freedom and seek release from traditional customs and institutions that enslave. The urge to build new patterns of society in which fundamental human rights, economic welfare and social well-being can be attained is widespread. . . . In this process of social reconstruction the search for new moral and spiritual foundations is basic, and the Christian understanding of man is directly relevant to the search for new foundations for society."[1]

Let us look more closely at some of the changes which are challenging us in the Christian Church.

Urbanisation and Industrialisation. Christian missions in most parts of the world have largely concentrated on the rural areas and the intelligentsia in the cities. These were obviously the places to begin when the missionaries first entered the country, and the link between them was the Christian school and college. Senior schools were established in central towns so that those of any religion who desired an English education in a Christian institution could get it, but even more so that the bright boys from the villages could continue their education and train as teachers or pastors and become leaders in the villages. What happened, of course, was that "city lights" and white-collar jobs with good pay frequently, for all but the most devoted, proved more attractive than a return to village conditions. They felt separated by their higher education from their village companions, and they also felt separated, perhaps partly by an uneasy conscience, from whatever Christian churches there might be in the town. Even more, those who came to the towns seeking work because of famine or loss of land or out of sheer poverty, would find church life in the city very different from anything they had known in the village. They were strangers in a congregation where everybody knew everybody. If not the denomination, then almost certainly the theology and possibly the language would be different, and in far too many cases they drifted away.

[1] World Council of Churches, Report of Central Committee, 1955.

A Pakistani once put it this way: "If the Communist Party wants to contact one of its members, no matter where he may be, in a few days it will have tracked him down. If the police want to put their hands on a suspect, they can immediately put the wheels in motion to lay hold of him. But if a Christian boy moves away from home, that is the last that the Church knows of him."

Some of the Christian missions in Kenya have been at work for many years, with considerable effect, in the rural areas, but had never followed their people when they moved to the city. Then it was discovered that the whole network of the Mau Mau movement was operated from Nairobi. Work which was being done in the villages was being undone in the cities. One of the main projects for contributing to the rebuilding of community life is therefore to be the establishment of five community centres staffed by the churches and Christian organisations in Nairobi itself.

Perhaps the most dramatic example of industrial revolution is in the Copper Belt of Central Africa. Here, says a pamphlet published in 1951, "where within living memory, the slave gangs struggled through the bush, vast industrial undertakings have sprung into being. Where the rural craftsman plied his trade, his sons work in smelter, shop and underground. And in place of the simple village community, vast compounds house the labour force at every mine."[1] Thousands of men trek in from the surrounding area, leaving their land to be cared for by their wives and families, while they contract for, perhaps, two years' service. Others come in on a monthly basis. While the mining companies, European owned and managed, provide welfare services of every kind, the disruption goes deeper. The London Missionary Society, which was already at work in this area when the mining development began, quickly realised that nothing

[1] In the Heart of Africa: 1951. London Committee of United Missions in the Copper Belt.

but a combined effort could begin to meet the needs and problems, inter-racial, social, economic, moral and spiritual, of both European and African. So the United Missions in the Copper Belt came into being, a joint enterprise comprising, among others, the London Missionary Society, Methodist Missionary Society, Church of Scotland, Universities Mission to Central Africa (Anglican), together with the United Society for Christian Literature. Roman Catholics co-operate in the educational work. Recently an African pastor has been appointed to specialise in work among adolescents, and an effort is being made to show the relevance of the Christian Faith for every aspect of life: in administration, in home, business, store and mine.

Just because this industrial development was on such an immense scale, it could not be overlooked. That this type of work is not more general wherever industry has been established is partly due to the weakness of the churches in that field in the "home" countries. One of the clearest developments in post-war church life in Britain and Europe has been the effort on the part of the churches to reach the industrial masses. As today in Asia and Africa, so in the last century in Britain, Europe and America, the population moved into the cities and the churches on the whole stayed in the country until city slums had been built and ways of life established. The result is that today, when the Church is aware of this danger abroad, it has not got the resources in experienced personnel to send out for industrial work that it has for evangelistic, educational or medical work. A leading American, reporting on a tour of Christian institutions in Africa some years ago, said that it would be his advice that the missions, given a choice, should abandon all their educational work and throw their people into the Trade Union movement. He believed that it was not in the primary schools, but in the rapidly developing industrial organisations that the battle for the soul of the nation would be fought out. But even if they had had the choice, it is doubtful whether the missionary societies would have been able to find the men with Christian conviction and experience of the Trade Union movement or real inside knowledge of workers' organisations who could have gone out to seize such an opportunity. So the boy trained in the mission school, perhaps even trained for a trade in a Christian Institute, all too often goes to the city for work. He is either scared by the kind of life he sees and retreats into loneliness, or fraternises with a like-minded group, maintaining an inner Christian faith which finds no appropriate expression, or else he decides that Christianity must wait until the struggle for political and economic freedom is won. He throws himself into the battle believing in the Christian Gospel—"but," like St. Augustine, "not now."

If the Church in the West cannot give a lead in this field, it can at least take the "younger churches" into its confidence, share with them the lessons it has learnt from its failures and its experiments, and give, especially to those lay Christians who come for industrial or technical training to the West and will go back to key positions in their countries, an opportunity to see and learn for themselves what impact and relevance the Church can have on our industrialised society.

Industrialisation has done more than drive people into crowded cities. It has altered the traditional means by which people acquire experience. In the stable village community, necessary knowledge and experience is largely passed down by word of mouth, custom and ritual from one generation to another. One could be versed in the traditions of the tribe, its history and lore, its religion and customs, one could till the land and exchange produce without being able to read.

The Protestant Christian tradition has always laid stress on the ability to read, so that each person could read the Bible for himself and not be dependent on hearsay for interpretation. The tendency therefore, when education has been part of missionary work, has been to emphasise book-learning rather than practical

53

knowledge. This fitted in well with the demand which grew up at the same time, for English-speaking clerks for government offices and business firms. These, together with teachers to expand the educational services, pastors to care for the churches and the small group of professional people, largely came from mission schools.

The industrial concerns demanded a different kind of knowledge—one that could not be passed down by the older generation, and had to be acquired by far greater numbers than could go through normal schooling. This is the ability to follow printed directions, to understand contracts, to negotiate agreements often between parties very unequal in skill and experience—a Western firm and native labour, for instance. The result, aided by mass literacy campaigns such as those for which Dr. Frank Laubach is famous, is a tremendous increase in mass literacy and an even greater increase in those who can be reached by mass-media such as radio and cinema because of concentrations of population in cities.

But what do these people read and see and hear? The people who best understand the use of mass-media because of the nature of the populations with which they work are the Communists. It only needs one literate person in a village or a factory to write a slogan on a wall and to read it out to all who stop and stare. One loud speaker can reach thousands of people at a time in the market place or at the factory gates. One small printing press can produce thousands of leaflets—probably with a crude but telling cartoon and the minimum of wording. This is entirely different from the Christian literary tradition, but it is clearly the literates from the mission schools who are most open to influence and most sought after by the Communists as workers and interpreters.

The Communists do not stop with the new literates. They are equally anxious to gain the intelligentsia, who are the great centres of influence in any community. No one has travelled far in recent years in Asia or Africa without being invited, on a train or at a railway station, to buy standard Communist works at give-away prices. Outside the entrance of the World Conference of Christian Youth at Kottayam in South India in 1952 was a Communist book-stall well stocked with books in English, staffed by volunteers who knew and understood the programme and purposes of the Conference and were ready to take on anyone in discussion.

Christian missionary bodies have become "communication conscious", not primarily to offset Communist propaganda, but because they have become aware that schools are not enough for the modern world. If they are concerned to teach people to read, they should equally be concerned as to what they read. If they are eager, through the schools, to give a Christian education and bring young people into the Christian Church, they should be equally concerned to keep them there as adults—and to help them to have adult convictions. So modern means of mass communication begin to figure more prominently in the work of the churches in all countries. The gramophone has always been a means of drawing a crowd. Now it is aided by the loud speaker. Much effort is spent in trying to secure "Christian time" on the radio. "Audio-visual aids" of all kinds—pictures, posters, strip cartoons, film strips, films—everything from the simplest to the most elaborate, may be part of the essential equipment of the evangelist. And RAVEMMCO (Radio, Visual Education and Mass Communication Committee) offers training scholarships in the United States for the increasing, if small, number of nationals who are able to specialise in this field.

Of all these media, literature is naturally the most developed. Dr. Frank Laubach has spent a lifetime in teaching people to read. He has awakened the conscience of churches and governments to the evils of illiteracy and his methods of teaching adults to read have been widely used. Now his son is devoting himself to teaching people to write, so that the "new literates" may have something of value to read. Syracuse University in the U.S.A. has special courses in its Department of Journalism on Writing for New Literates. People are sent there to train from many parts of the world. Many return to their own countries, notably to India and the Philippines, to conduct their own schools of Christian Journalism.

In Japan for many years, "newspaper evangelism" has been carried on. Japan is the most literate country in the East, but it has one of the proportionately smallest Christian communities. If the Christians are to reach beyond their immediate contacts, they must use more than personal methods. Notices giving an address to which enquirers may write for Christian information have proved immensely fruitful—but literature has to be written to follow up contacts.

China is now closed to foreign work, but millions of Chinese live in Hong Kong, Formosa, Borneo, Malaya, Thailand, Indonesia—where the primary concern of the missionaries is not always with the Chinese-speaking population. To help meet this problem and also to make full use of all the available resources for Chinese evangelism, a Council on Christian Literature for Overseas Chinese has been set up, operating from Hong Kong, but serving the wide Chinese dispersion outside China.

A special Committee[1] has long been working on Christian Literature for Africa, and early discovered that the story is not finished when people have been taught to read, and books have been written. There is the further problem of bringing the books to the people. So a Book-Room becomes an essential part of a new centre for Christian work in the Copper Belt, and Book Vans are added to missionary equipment in many parts of Africa.

This task of providing Christian literature is a clear case for working co-operatively. This principle is being carried out to

[1] International Council on Christian Literature for Africa, 2 Eaton Gate, London, S.W.1.

the full in the present venture of World Christian Books.[1] Sponsored by the International Missionary Council and supported by British, American and Canadian Mission Boards, authors of many Christian denominations and nationalities are writing short books in simple but adult language on the main themes of the Christian faith. The aim is to provide a basic library which can be easily adapted into many languages and will provide those who teach the Church's faith, especially those with little theological training, with sound material of practical value.

But literature still has a hard struggle to be recognised as one of the most powerful missionaries the Church possesses, able to travel where no evangelist can go, able to reach thousands of people who never enter a Christian building, able to build up and encourage and strengthen in the faith those who are given responsibility in the Church and have very often so little in the way of stimulus or guidance for the difficult task of commending the Gospel in a way relevant to the modern world.

"Disturbing a pattern of life" is too mild a form of words to use for the revolution that has come to the lives of many of the people of Malaya and Kenya.

In the Federation of Malaya more than half the population are immigrant Chinese. While the Malays live in village communities, the Chinese peasant farmers tended to live in isolated homesteads on the edge of the jungle. From them the Communist groups gained their recruits—often by intimidation—and on them the Communists living in hiding in the jungle, depended for food supplies. In order to protect these peasants as well as to cut off supplies from the Communists, the Government decided in 1951 to move these isolated families into villages where they would be under armed protection. Imagine the dismay when soldiers arrived with orders that in two days (some-

[1] *World Christian Books,* English edition, Nos. 1-12, published by the Lutterworth Press, 2s. 6d.

times without even this warning), families were to be ready to move, with what belongings they had and as much wood from the house as was movable. Transported by army lorry, they were then taken to a huge enclosure surrounded by a double fence of barbed wire. For the first few days they might be given shelter along with hundreds of other families, in huge wooden huts. Material was provided for them to put up their own houses, a site being allocated on one of the "streets". Then, once established, they were free either to continue to care for their land if it was not too far away, or to find work as rubber tappers.

While the Government was responsible for the move, it realised that the job was not finished by physically transplanting 400,000 of the population into 400 villages. The villages could themselves very easily become centres of disaffection and of anti-Government agitation. To do the job properly, the people must learn the positive advantages of village life, must be introduced to community organisation and helped to establish themselves as a neighbourhood. To do this, the Government appointed Welfare Officers who in turn looked to every agency which might win the confidence of the people and help them to take a positive attitude to their enforced new mode of existence. Naturally they turned to the missionaries as a group already on the field and already in touch with the Chinese, most of them speaking one or other of the Chinese dialects.

Here was a problem. The Christian missionaries had had to leave China largely under the charge of being the agents, or tools, or "stooges" of their Governments. Many had come to work in Malaya determined not to repeat the mistakes which they believed had been made in China. Yet here was an invitation to start new work at Government request, a great deal of which would inevitably involve interpreting the policy of the Government in a good light. And if on grounds of policy they refused? Not only would an unprecedented opportunity for reaching the Chinese go by, but the attempt would have to be made by other agencies, educational, welfare, social, to build up community life according to their best insights while the Church, which is said to have the secret of "community", stood aside. They could not refuse, but they could at least show by their lives and actions that they cared first and foremost for the good of the village people. They could take the very charge of being agents of Government as an opportunity to show that the Christian Church is not a mere Department of State. By working in international teams including Chinese members and by living themselves in the villages, so that their manner of life was open for public inspection, they could hope to convey to these bewildered people that there were those who cared for them as people, not just as part of the anti-Communist strategy.

In order to begin this task, the churches and Christian forces in Malaya had to face with a new sense of its relevance and urgency the fact of their own divisions. They could not try to build up community life and at the same time introduce Christian divisions. However they acted, there must be unity and common policy among Christians. The main churches, Anglican, Methodist, Presbyterian, were already working together in the Malayan Christian Council, but their forces were not strong enough to meet the new demand. Societies, some of which, like the China Inland Mission, had not taken part in Christian co-operation in China itself, were anxious to send workers. An agreement had to be made that there should be no rivalry or competition but that in each village the attempt would be made to build up one Christian community.

But was even this enough? Has the Church really the secret of community life? Has it not succeeded in winning people *away* from their natural communities rather than helping them to take responsibility *in* them? Was not part of the charge against the Church in China that it created coteries of Christians who were out of touch with the social needs of their communities? Here and there Christians gave a lead in organising co-operatives and helping to find a solution to social problems, but on the whole they dealt with individuals rather than social units.

Not only in China but throughout the world, the Church has been seeking to recover what it means to be in the world for the sake of the world—not identified with it nor regardless of it. There are very few Christians in these new villages. They are mainly simple people—not necessarily the natural leaders. How are they to be trained in their understanding of the Christian way of life, and how is the Christian impact to be brought to bear on the village as a whole? This is the same problem that is being faced in the villages of England, where the Church has lost touch with the community, in the industrial areas, where it has too rarely been a formative influence, as well as in the larger area of the State. It is not that the West has the answers and takes them to the East, but that in this new day in which God has faced us with so many unprecedented situations, the Church seeks to listen and to learn by experiment and experience into what new paths God is leading it.

What happened in Malaya gave a clue to those who were faced with a similar problem in Kenya. There too the people lived in separated farmsteads, which gave the Mau Mau the opportunity to intimidate people, and to carry out their ceremonies in isolated places without arousing suspicion. The Government decided to move all suspects into detention camps, and then agreed that, even when they were cleared, they should not be allowed to return to the same style of life, but should be put into villages and taught the ways of community life.

As in Malaya, the appeal was made to the churches to help them to establish themselves, and the same problem arose of the churches, if they agreed, apparently giving evidence that they were on the side of the Government against which the Mau Mau were rebelling. The number of Christians involved was considerably greater than in Malaya, but the bitterness and distrust were also far greater. Again, the only way the Church found to meet the need of the people without identifying itself with Government was to act internationally—to appeal, not just to British Churches, but to the World Council of Churches. It was asked to put at the service of the Christian Church in Kenya the experience it had had elsewhere in Refugee and Emergency work and to send internationally recruited personnel, especially those with understanding of community problems. In this way not only was the basis of recruitment widened, but the opportunity was given to interpret the Church to the Kikuyu as a world-wide body, of which they were a part.

The family is the basic unit in any society. When family life begins to disintegrate, it is a sure sign that a society is on the down grade. When a society is broken up by war or any kind of revolution, the family suffers. As things look at the present day, the family is suffering both from the decay of the old societies and the impact of the new.

A Burmese writer tells how contact with the West has had a double effect on his country. On the one hand it has brought about a strong sense of nationalism, bound together by the Buddhist faith. On the other, it has caused some of the most sacred traditions of Buddhist life to be challenged from within. Among these traditions are those of the respect and honour due to the parent and the teacher. "There have been wholesale questionings," he says, "of the prevailing parental authority on a number of matters and also of the basis of the pupil-teacher relationship. Cartoons, novels, dramas, songs and films caricature the blatant departures of the present from the past and the awkward characteristics of the new relationships."

From Japan, also, with its traditional society of "vertical relationships", where everyone knew his place in relation to his superiors and inferiors, the question is that of remodelling the social system, including the whole conception of the family.

But on what basis is family life to be remodelled? Not that of the migratory labour of South Africa, where thousands of men leave their land to be tended by the women and move into the locations for perhaps two years at a time. Many of the firms may provide good living quarters and welfare facilities, but they are at the same time destroying the basis of society in the family.

Nor can the family be re-modelled on the lines of Western family life as portrayed by the movies and magazines, which is the only picture that most people in Asia and Africa have of the—to them—"Christian" West.

If the Christian Church is to make any contribution to building up strong, happy family life and a new society of healthy relationships, it has to fight on two fronts—both against the crumbling conservatism of the old forms and the laxity of the new.

The question of family life has more than one aspect to it. It involves, for example, the position given to women in the home and in society, the relations of the older and younger generations, the ways in which young people find—or have found for them—their marriage partner, the training and discipline of children, family activities and responsibilities, and the relation of the family to the Church and the wider society. All these aspects were touched on in a recent conference on Christian Family Life held in the Philippines with delegates from ten East Asian countries and invited guests and speakers from India, U.S.A. and Great Britain.

This Conference brought together those who have been active in establishing the Christian Home Movement in these countries.

The Movement began in China and spread to India, where it took firm root. When Miss Irma Highbaugh, an American missionary and a national secretary of the movement in China, had to leave that country, she was asked by the International Missionary Council to spend time in each of the countries of East Asia, working with Christian groups on these questions. This Conference was a milestone in the development of Christian action in this field.

Delegates from each country told of the revolt of youth against authority, of their desire to choose their own jobs and their own marriage partners. They told of the puzzlement of the old people, unable to understand the new world which had appeared so suddenly around them. They told of confusion in relation to standards of sex relationships. They expressed their doubts about the Western "single unit family", where a man and his wife set up house on their own, in comparison with the Asian joint family system, where a man brings his wife to his own home, and they live as a "sub-family" in a larger community of grand-parents, aunts, uncles and cousins—thus avoiding, at the least, the need for seeking baby-sitters and the loneliness of the only child!

"Neither parents nor children know what to keep from the old nor what to select from the new in order to bring about the good life," says the Conference Report.[1] It is just here that the Christian understanding of human nature and personality can be "good news" . . . but that is something which has to be learnt in and by the Church before it can be told and shown to non-Christian neighbours.

Jesus' courtesy towards women and friendship with women has revolutionised for Christians many traditional ideas which are still maintained in non-Christian societies. One of the out-standing contributions of Christian missions has been to intro-duce women's education and to open up spheres of service and responsibility for women. It can be the proud boast of Christian missions in India that two of her main teaching hospitals—Ludhiana in the North and Vellore in the south—were founded by women for women. And where would any medical service be if nursing had not been introduced as an expression of Christian service? In many churches of Asia and Africa women play a relatively greater and more responsible part than they do in many churches of the West.

[1] Christian Family Life Conference. International Missionary Council.

But respect for personality in women means a great many adjustments on the part of men. It is of the whole world and not primarily of the Asian countries that a Department of the World Council of Churches is thinking when it undertakes to study "the co-operation of men and women in church and society." This is an uneasy question in most parts of the world, but while the West is perhaps used to making its adjustments slowly, Africa and the East need to know *now* where they are going, so as not to have to unlearn their mistakes—or mistakes which they have taken over from the West—later on.

So with the relations between young men and women. The West is used to its young people mixing freely, working and playing together. We believe that, even if it has its dangers, this is the way that young people will get to know and respect one another and gain the knowledge of the other sex which will help them to find a marriage partner, or to lead a satisfying life as single men or women. In the confidence that this is universally true, we have introduced co-education into countries where it is an entirely new idea and looked on with considerable hesitation by the old generation. We are beginning to learn that it is not enough, anywhere, just to bring young people together. They must at the same time be given Christian teaching (and those who are keenest on co-education are not always prepared to see that the consequence must be explicit teaching on the Christian understanding of sex and the relations of the sexes) and the strong support of Christian fellowship. Where this has been done with conviction and courage, it has often given new heart to the Christian community. In Pakistan, for example, the Christian women are constantly under criticism from the Muslims because they go about with their faces uncovered. After much hesitation and consultation a team of men and women students decided to work together to establish a youth centre in the hills. The experience of sharing together in manual work, in meals and study, in worship and in recreation, has transformed many of them from being hesitant members of a minority to people who know the strength and joy of Christian community and are eager to share it with others.

"Relationship" is the present popular emphasis in theology. We are persons, we are told, only as we are in relation with other people—children with parents, man with wife, friend with friend, and all of us with God. The place to discover this is in the Christian family. Yet so much of Christian life in a non-Christian country has tended to be negative—*not* going to the temple, *not* taking part in non-Christian festivals, *not* conforming to the surrounding customs. Now, in India especially, the Christian Home Movement is encouraging families, in their own circles and in the wider circle of the Church, to make the Christian Festivals times of doing-things-together, showing that to Christ every member of the family, from the oldest to the youngest, is important and has his part to play.

This secret of life-in-community is as relevant to the atomised Western families, where there are separate organisations even in the church for each member of the family, as to the joint families of the East, where perhaps too much wisdom is expected to reside with age. Just as the churches of East Asia learnt from one another in Conference, so may the "individualist" West learn from the "corporate" East, within the world-wide family of Christ's Church.

E

V

"In the likeness of men"

"Have this mind in you which was also in Christ Jesus, who, though he was in the form of God, did not count equality with God a thing to be grasped, but emptied himself, taking the form of a servant, being born in the likeness of men. And being found in human form he humbled himself and became obedient unto death, even death on a cross." (Phil. 2: 5, 6, 8)

Jesus, Son of God, King of the Jews as he knew himself to be, lived and died as a man of Galilee. So much was he identified with the life of his time that people could not believe that what he claimed could be true. Even John the Baptist, who was the first to hail him and to baptise him for his ministry, sent from prison to ask, "Art thou he that should come or look we for another?" The more Jesus did the works of God in healing and teaching and preaching, the more the scribes and Pharisees asked him for a sign, a miracle, something startling, that would convince them in spite of themselves. And among his own people there were those who took offence at the idea of the village carpenter's son setting up to teach others.

The Church is often concerned about questions of status and public recognition, but its real concern should be that which is shown by Paul in the passage quoted above from the letter to the Philippians—to be among men as one of them, as the humblest among them. Jesus did not come to the people of Palestine as a foreigner but as one of themselves: "he came to his own home" (John 1: 11 R.S.V.). One of the tasks laid upon the Church today as it reaches out to the whole world is to learn how to live among men of any and every country—as theirs, not a foreign

66

*import, and yet at the same time to be the Church of Jesus
Christ, serving his will and not subservient to the will of men.*

A GROUP of British young people were describing Christmas
to a foreigner. They told about the singing of carols;
decorating the house with holly; plum-puddings and Christmas
dinner, Santa Claus and present-giving. Yet how much of this is
strictly Christian?

Go back in imagination to the days when the first missionaries
were at work in Britain. Think of the arguments that might
have gone on among the early converts from the worship of
Wotan and Thor. Should mistletoe be allowed in Church? Was
it sacrilege to put Christian words to heathen tunes? What happened to Christian truth when the Christians began celebrating
the birth of Christ at the time of the heathen rites connected
with the depth of winter?

Yet so thoroughly have we lost any awareness of the original
religious significance of holly and mistletoe and any *lack* of
Christian significance in plum-pudding, that when we go abroad
we take these irrelevances with us. On Christmas Eve in India,
with the stars blazing in a sky of deep blue, with the watchmen's
fires making a glow to light up the village huts and everything
as like the first Christmas Eve as it could be, Britishers have
been heard complaining, "It doesn't seem a real Christmas
without snow," and little Indian children have been seen busily
and painstakingly copying robins (a bird they have never seen)
and holly leaves from old Christmas cards and painting them
on the walls of their huts—conveying nothing at all to their
non-Christian neighbours!

In other words, Christmas has become so *indigenised* in Britain
that we find it hard to distinguish the essential Christian from
other elements—those which originally belonged to another
religious tradition (such as mistletoe and candles) and those which
are purely local—snow and robins.

Come to a church service in West Africa. It is a day of tropical steamy heat. We come through a village where the people live in grass-thatched huts or in light wooden houses. Men and women are wearing bright coloured robes. When we arrive in the town for church, we go into a stone, Gothic style building with wooden benches. The men, to our surprise, wear black cloth suits and stiff collars. The minister has a dog collar and preaching gown. If this is a Presbyterian Church and it is a special occasion, the Moderator may be present, wearing the three-cornered hat, the lace fall and cuffs and the knee breeches which are still moderatorial wear in Scotland! The tunes are probably those we would hear in our own churches. We notice that the words are in the African language, but we may not know that, set to that kind of music the African words lose their meaning! We begin to understand the amazement of a West African student in America as he saw people going to church in their ordinary clothes. "Why," he said, "here the church is indigenised!"

The early missionaries had no desire or intention to plant foreign churches. It was because of their passionate conviction that Christ's message was for the whole world that they went abroad at all. But they were determined that the churches they established and the communities that accepted the Gospel should be *Christian*. They believed that a clean break had to be made with the past so that the next generation would not even know the meaning of heathen ceremonies. They wanted to express the new life in outward forms which were themselves new. They could not, with their limited knowledge and experience of the life of the people they were among, invent new forms in, so to speak, the local idiom, so they gave what they knew and what they could themselves interpret. And they succeeded. Churches were established which are now strong enough to be producing their own leaders. In many cases they are becoming autonomous churches, making their own decisions. If missionaries share in those decisions, it is as members of the Church, with no special power or authority. Here then too is a point where much reconsideration and reassessment is needed if the Church is to be truly Christian, truly "indigenous" and truly universal.

The nationalist criticism of missionary-founded churches is that they are "spiritual colonies of the West"[1], or, to use a phrase of D. T. Niles of Ceylon, "potted plants", transferred but not yet adapted to the soil and climate of a new country. These phrases may cause pain to those who have given their lives to the transplanting process, but they may also be a serious reminder not to stop half-way in the task of "identification" which is given by Christ himself.

The traveller abroad, missionary or otherwise, is frequently much impressed by the forms of devotion which he observes among the devotees of other religions. He sees the Hindu woman bringing flowers to the local shrine, hears the Buddhist monks chanting in the temple, and is shamed by the Muslim's faithfulness to the hours of prayer. In comparison, he may find Christian worship unromantic. But what does he know of the spiritual reality which lies behind these outward forms? Unconsciously, someone with a Christian tradition, seeing the form of reverence or prayer, fills it with Christian content. But those who came out from these religions because these leaders had found the Truth as it is in Jesus Christ wanted to express their new life in totally new forms, distinct from those of the old religion. For them the Gothic churches, wooden benches and hymn tunes of the Westerner carried only Christian associations. It was a later generation which discovered that they were "Western". An Englishman may be startled and shocked or amused according to temperament, to hear the strains of "Clementine" during a Punjabi church service and find it set to the words of a Psalm. "Clementine" has associations of a non-religious nature for him but not for them. Church authorities of one of the Indonesian

[1] See article by D. G. Moses, N.C.C. Review (India), March 1955.

islands forbade the singing of Christian hymns to Hindu melodies, not because they were old-fashioned, but because of the associations, still powerful, with the baser elements of Hindu worship which these melodies carried.

But this is not a static situation and every country learns to distinguish, as in ancient Britain, between what is local, what can be used of old religious custom and what is essentially Christian. Taking India again as an example, it is increasingly accepted that in matters like slipping off shoes and sitting on the floor or wearing shoes and sitting on chairs, each congregation does what is most natural. Indian music and songs and lyrics are very widely used as Indian poets express in their own forms their love for Christ. In the South, where the Christian community is comparatively strong and well-rooted, Old and New Testament stories have been set to old folk-dance tunes and are sung and danced by village people. The lit lamp is much used in Hinduism, but it is also one of the most ancient Christian symbols. To use it, as is increasingly done, is to fill it with Christian meaning.

So with architecture. Some of the most successful and satisfying adaptations of native styles of architecture for Christian buildings, such as the Cathedral at Dornakal in South India and some of the Christian college chapels there and in Ceylon, have in fact been inspired by missionary leadership, but have now proved themselves and are setting the example for other experiments.

The missionary has often been accused of "foreignness" and this is indeed inevitable in some degree. But often it has been the missionary who has taken the initiative in making the outward accompaniments of Christian worship more truly indigenous, while his national colleagues have clung to the more western ways of expression. There is a telling illustration of this in the experience of a missionary in Burma, who with the acquiescence of his congregation, banished pews, pulpit, kneeling desks, offertory bags from the church building, only to find some months later that they had been salvaged by a Burmese colleague to embellish a rather bare church building some miles away.

Christian artists are also beginning to interpret the Gospel story in ways that will appeal to their own people.[1] One of the boldest of these artists in India is Alfred David Thomas, for, by his pictures, he carries the Christian claim right into the popular Hindu mythology. In a picture of Christ in an Indian village he portrays Christ, followed like any Holy Man of the East by one disciple and the disciple carries a trident. This three-pronged fork is to be seen stuck in the ground beside any Hindu shrine. It symbolises in Hindu thought Brahma, the Creator, Vishnu, the Preserver, and Siva, the Destroyer. Yet in the Christian disciple's hand it stands for the Christian Trinity, Father, Son and Holy Ghost. Among the crowd in the village street is a kneeling widow, offering Jesus the lotus, the flower of India. Another woman on her way to the temple, turns aside to look and listen. A saffron-robed priest is shown eagerly seeking for greater truth than he has yet found. A young student hovers in the background. And two young men wearing Gandhi caps are in the crowd, one frankly interested, another turning his head away. So the artist seeks, in a way that Indians can immediately understand, to show Christ saying to all Hindu India, literate and illiterate, rich and poor, "Come unto me and I will give you rest." The poets too express their longing that India should welcome the Saviour of the world:

> "Our wise men have not yet seen the star
> and the manger of Bethlehem
> is not yet the cradle of our land.
> But Christian hope never dies
> and the ends of the strands of destiny
> are held safe in the hands of God."[2]

[1] *The Life of Christ* and *In Parables*, illustrations of the Parables of Christ by Chinese artists. S.P.G.
[2] Chandran Devanesen: *The Cross is Lifted.*

We said earlier that the Church must be truly Christian, truly indigenous and *truly universal*. There is a temptation to become so "indigenised" as to forget that all Christians, of whatever race or nation, have a common heritage. It was an Indian who said, "The *Messiah* is part of my Christian inheritance." As we open our own hymn books, we are often unaware of the wealth that is contained there, drawn from churches of many nations and centuries. We must not impoverish the "younger churches" and deny them their right to share this heritage with us, but we must also welcome into our ways of worship some of the riches that will increasingly come to us from them. The aim stated in the Constitution of the Church of South India, "to express under Indian conditions and Indian forms, the spirit, thought and life of the Church Universal," should, in its own situation, be the aim of every Church.

That there are still wider problems involved than those of forms of worship is shown by a Conference called in May 1955 by the National Christian Council of the Gold Coast on the subject of *Christian Faith and African Culture*. Here they were not dealing with comparatively simple questions such as speaking and preaching in the vernacular rather than in English, or wearing African dress. They were facing the fact, felt intensely both by Africans and missionaries, that Christianity has not yet bitten deep enough into African life.

While there may be Christian profession and outward conformity, there is still unresolved conflict between the African and the Christian understanding of life. Or, as many of them are asking, is this not rather a conflict between an African and a *Western* understanding of life? Especially at this time when West Africa is moving rapidly towards self-government, Christians are painfully aware of being cut off from many of the expressions of the African spirit and of nationhood. An observer from the West, commenting on this Conference, described how urgent this topic had become:

"In the present situation of nationalist feeling and sentiment, there is a tendency to revive African customs, including African religious customs, such as the pouring of libations to ancestors. At various social and political meetings, such as the election of a chief, such libations are poured. Christians have not participated in such ceremonies, but they are beginning to feel the need to show their national loyalty and their loyalty to African customs. . . . The question was what attitude should Christians take to ancestor worship, witchcraft, fetishism, etc. Such points were very seriously and lengthily debated in the search for some way round the conflict between Christian faith and African beliefs."

Closely involved with this question is an even more far-reaching one. Does evangelism, as normally practised by missionaries from the West, reach the whole of a man's being? Does conversion cover his whole understanding of life, in all its heights and depths, or does it only touch him partially? The story of Made, type of the Hindus of Bali, one of the Indonesian islands, illustrates this problem. In essence it is in the minds of those considering rural evangelism in any part of the world.

"Made is entirely at home in the Hindu world of Bali. In his courtyard there is the usual little family temple, where his wife makes the daily sacrifice at sunset. He plays in the village orchestra which frequently performs for the temple rites. He is proud when he sees his daughter dancing there.

"Although Made is illiterate, he knows by heart the long Hindu poems. He has an answer for the deepest problems of life: sickness and death, fertility and misfortune. He knows the whole Hindu mythology and cosmology of Bali.

"But for some time Made has not been too secure in this world outlook. From travelling Chinese he has heard stories of a great teacher, Jesus, who died for him. He has learnt some simple hymns about salvation. . . . All this struck home to Made's heart. He wanted to become a Christian."

The story then goes on to show what it means to come out of such a thought world and become a Christian: "The first thing that is necessary in preparing Made to become a Christian is to free him from the spell of the conception of the world based on naturalistic myths. These old stories explain the present breach between the ideal conditions of earliest times and the present situation full of suffering. They are the framework in which Made sees everything which has happened, happens or could happen.

"Therefore if we pass on to him Bible stories and a few fragments of Christian dogmas and ethics, he will quite unconsciously fit all this into the framework of his Hindu mythology. Unconsciously he will give Christ a mythical form and add him to the heirachy of the good mountain gods which fight against the demons of the sea. And Christ will no longer be the Biblical historical Christ, "crucified under Pontius Pilate." In spite of all his Christian knowledge, Made will remain a heathen.

"So the most important thing is to replace this closed circle of mythology with quite a new—Biblical—understanding of the world and of its history. The drama of salvation in the Bible beginning with the creation and fall and ending with the coming Kingdom of God, with Christ as the determining centre and turning point has to become the background of all his thinking. Answers to the problems of sickness and death, fertility and misfortune, have to be found in Biblical terms. He must learn to understand this not as "foreign teaching", but as the answer of the living God to the mystery of the universe and he must find his place in this divine drama.

"He and his family will give up the sunset sacrifices, but instead they will meet morning and evening for Christian worship. For the present he will give up playing in the village orchestra, for that would be to live in two worlds. But the time may come when he will be making music to express the words of the Psalms in his own language or to accompany the Bible stories.

"In this way he must expect to find himself with a God-given task to confront the mythology of his own village with the story of God's mighty acts. He must take his share in putting before his village the challenge of decision, but he will do this naturally, because it has soaked into his entire being."[1]

What should be happening in the villages of Bali and its equivalent in every land, should be happening also in a true confrontation between Christianity and the higher cultures. "A deadlock isolates the Church from cultured India," says an Indian Christian. "And it is a deadlock which prevents the Indian nation from listening to the Divine Word which alone can judge and redeem its cultural tradition and convert it into a true foundation for the new society which Free India is called upon to build to-day."

How can this deadlock be broken, so that the new countries of Asia and Africa may be truly shaped and re-made by the Word of God? It may be that one way to help this is for the churches of the West to become more aware of the extent to which they have allowed the Church to be embedded in their culture so that they cannot distinguish between Christianity and their particular way of life. While the Church in every land must be deeply involved in the life and fate and destiny of that country, it must always be the Church of Jesus Christ, Son of God as well as Son of Man. We have too easily agreed with those who talk about the "Christian West" as if we believed that our national life was truly and wholly under obedience to the will of God in Christ. We have forgotten that Christ is Judge as well as King and so being confused ourselves, we have brought confusion to those to whom we meant only to commend the Gospel.

[1] Adapted from an address by Hans Rudi Weber to the Basel Mission, by permission.

75

East and West together, we need to learn to live as those Christians described in the Epistle to Diognetus:

"Christians are not distinguished from the rest of mankind either in locality or in speech or in customs. . . . They dwell in their own countries, but only as sojourners; they bear their share in all things as citizens and they endure all hardships as strangers . . . . Every foreign country is a fatherland to them and every fatherland is foreign. . . . They obey the established laws, and they surpass the laws in their own lives. . . . In a word, what the soul is in the body, this the Christians are in the world."

VI

"And with him two others"

In St. John's story of the Crucifixion there is an extraordinary touch of insight and delicacy. While every other Gospel speaks of Jesus being crucified "between two thieves" (Matt. and Mark), or "between two malefactors" (Luke), John writes only of "two others". In this way he minimises, not the sin of those who were crucified, but their separateness from the ordinary run of human kind. To John the contrast between Jesus and humanity was so great, that the difference between men in general and two who were being punished for some offence against Rome seemed insignificant. "There, but for the grace of God . . ."

Jesus was identified with the sin of men in his death as he had been in his baptism. Himself without sin, he could go with these wrong-doers into the depth of their experience—even to the depth of feeling forsaken by God—and yet he could take them, if they repented to the height of his communion with the Father: "To-day ye shall be with me in paradise."

The Church, human and divine, is doubly identified with those "two others", for while it goes among suffering and sinful mankind to seek and to save, in the Name of Christ, it is itself involved in the sinful situation: "The evil that I would not that I do." With Paul, we can thank God for the Cross of Redemption: "Who shall deliver me from this body of death? Thanks be to God, through Jesus Christ our Lord" (Rom. 7: 19, 24-5).

77

NOWHERE is the agony of the Church so clearly seen as in Africa. Is it possible to see, amid the conflict and torment of that Continent, three crosses, "on either side one, and Jesus in the midst"?

The group of young people who attended the youth conference preceding the Evanston Assembly of the World Council of Churches could believe that they had a glimpse of this very thing. A whole day was spent trying to understand and enter into the problems of Africa. A young Afrikaner spoke first, describing how his people had first gone to settle in South Africa, how they had tried to deal fairly with the tribes who were in possession of the land, honourably buying it from them; how they had developed and settled the land until it had become their own country, yet had always felt responsible for the Africans with whom they shared it; and he quoted the extent to which taxation benefited the native Africans in education, health services and so on. Immediately after him a young Bantu spoke. With equal skill, quietness and courtesy he told the same story from the point of view of his own people. He told how the early settlers had come to buy land from the native Africans, but did not understand that land was inalienable and could not be bought and sold, how they had been received with courtesy by the chiefs, but had been heard moving around among the huts after dark—a thing which could only mean evil to an African and so they had been killed—with the result that the white man had avenged the death of his fellows and fear and suspicion had been established between the two races. The same story, but how differently told and re-told down the generations by each of the races! So with the Bantu interpretation of Afrikaner concern for their welfare. While the Afrikaner saw how much had been done, the Bantu saw how little had been accomplished in comparison with the need, and above all, it was done as the white man determined and not as the Africans wished.

Then came another African, youngest son of the third wife

of a chief, who had come from an adjoining territory to study in the Union of South Africa and after some time had been required to leave without reason given. Following on these three, a young man from Kenya, a Kikuyu, spoke about some of the unrest that lay behind the Mau Mau rebellion—again the problem of land, which meant so much to the African and which to the European was a commodity to exchange for money.

What a miracle it was that these problems which divided race from race so bitterly within the one country, could be spoken of freely and sincerely within the Christian fellowship, and what a tragedy that the conflict in South Africa should be not merely between races but between churches.

Men do not wilfully create evil situations. The first Dutch settlers were men of God, with a profound sense of responsibility for the native Africans. Still, the work of the Dutch Reformed Church among Africans far outstrips anything being done by any other missionary body. Then came the British. The Boer War between Afrikaner and British settlers created a bitterness and antagonism which has never in seventy years been healed. South African politics and church relations would not be so difficult today if more British had taken the trouble to learn the language of the Afrikaner and to enter more sympathetically into his understanding of the Christian faith. So by allowing an unreconciled relationship to continue, the Church was weakened when it came to a real theological discussion of the place of the African in the new society. On the one side are those Afrikaners (and others) who maintain, on the grounds of their interpretation of the Scriptures, that their God-given duty is to maintain Christian civilisation in South Africa on the basis of white supremacy. And it must be sadly admitted that there are a large number of English-speaking South Africans who in their hearts support the policy of apartheid, though probably not on theological grounds. On the other side are those, African and some white, who deny that races are differently endowed by God and destined to develop separately or in different ways and who hold that the present policy of "differential development" is a denial of human rights.

So the bitter struggle goes on, with education transferred from the Ministry of Education to the Ministry of Native Affairs, indicating that education for Europeans is in a different class from that for Africans and destined to serve different ends; with the clearance of Africans out of white areas, which the Bishop of Johannesburg has denounced as, not slum clearance but "legalised theft"; and the increase in migratory labour, leading to the breakdown of family life and the evil effects of this, both in the cities where the men are crowded and in the rural areas where their families continue to live without them.

But even in this situation where it is said that every white South African, whatever his political beliefs, carries the burden of unhappiness and a sense of guilt, we can see signs that "Jesus is in the midst", sharing the suffering but also seeking to redeem it. There are many church leaders, not alone those who "hit the headlines" of the British Press, who have taken upon themselves, in Christ's Name, the cause of the Africans and are fighting by every permissible means for a society in which human rights, regardless of race or colour, shall be recognised. There is the Wilgespruit community—a Christian Conference centre built by young people themselves in inter-racial work camps, where those of any race or church can come together for Christian fellowship and grow in understanding each other and their Christian task. There are Race Relations Councils and other signs, of which the conversation with which this chapter opened was an example. The isolation, spiritual and geographical, of the churches in South Africa from one another is gradually being broken down.

A few leaders in the Dutch Reformed Church, with considerable courage, have been prepared to enter into conversation with fellow-Christians of other churches, to give and receive criticism before God and on the basis of His Word and to re-examine at least the theological arguments for the present political policy. This has led to the conference called by two Synods of the Dutch Reformed Church on the theme "The extension of the Kingdom of God in multi-racial South Africa." All the main denominations except the Roman Catholics were represented, membership was multi-racial and both the Afrikaner and English languages were used (while most Europeans used one or other, most Africans were at home in both!) The conference did not resolve differences, but it at least stressed that these things must be faced *within* the Christian community. It also lead to the decision to begin to work out certain tasks together—inter-racially. In the process of working together, deeper understanding can grow and defensive positions can be dropped. Something similar has happened within the fellowship of the World Council of Churches. Certain of the Dutch Reformed Churches of South Africa were received into membership of the Council at Evanston. Their delegates came, knowing that the only basis of membership was acceptance of our Lord Jesus Christ as God and Saviour. Knowing this, they knew that on many other matters they would not be at one with their fellow members in the Council. They took part in the discussion on Inter-group relations and expressed their views forcibly and freely. That section of the Assembly produced a report which declared the conviction of the Assembly "that any form of segregation based on race, colour or ethnic origin is contrary to the gospel and is incompatible with the Christian doctrine of men and with the nature of the Church of Christ. It urges the churches within its membership to renounce all forms of segregation or discrimination and to work for their abolition within their own life and within society." Such a statement was received without protest by the South African delegates as the voice of the Assembly and they undertook to take it back to their own churches and raise it for discussion and study. A

F

small thing in view of the immensity and urgency of the problem? Certainly, but a triumph of God's grace over human resistance to correction.

Is there time for change to come about as slowly as men's hearts are willing to change? That we do not know, but we can thank God for the miracle of African patience and forbearance up to the present and pray that we may buy up the time that remains to work for a change of policy which may "secure for all the opportunities for the free exercise of responsible citizenship and for effective participation in government" (Evanston Report). At the same time, we can learn our own lesson from this of the consequences of allowing lack of understanding and sympathy to grow up and to continue between and within churches. When the testing time comes, we are unable to meet it as Christians. As the Message of the First Assembly said, "As we have talked with each other, we have begun to understand how our separation has prevented us from receiving correction from one another in Christ. And because we lacked this correction, the world has often heard from us not the Word of God but the words of men."

Inevitably what has happened in South Africa has had a profound effect on the rest of the continent. South African race policy has crept into Southern Rhodesia and given the Africans of Northern Rhodesia and Nyasaland cause to fear that Federation will mean its extension northwards. Those who think only in political terms probably little realise that the history of Nyasaland is the history of the Christian missionary work there. Following Livingstone himself, the missionaries were for the greater part from Scotland, and the Africans, working from the known to the unknown, looked to Scotland—and therefore to Britain and British Government as the source of everything good and progressive. Nyasaland was made a Protectorate not as part of the scramble for land, but at the request of African church leaders and Christian traders, to protect it from encroachment by Portuguese East Africa. Regular treaties were made between Government and chiefs, and African leaders were associated with Government and policy making from the start. Therefore, it was natural that the Africans, finding themselves forced against their will into Federation, interpreted this as betrayal by the Church. They fear that their land will be taken by white immigrants, that the Protectorate status in which they have shared will give way to European rule and that the segregation which they have never known will creep up from the South.

Their confidence in the Church was such that they believed that the churches in Britain could have prevented Federation if they had wished. This was in fact an issue on which Christian opinion in Britain was roused as it has rarely been, but unsuccessfully. This failure is looked upon by the Africans as a betrayal of their interests by those whom they had believed to be friends. It has convinced them of what they had been told—that the missionary always sides with those of his own race—and has led to bitterness and frustration which may be serious both for the Church and for the political future.

This situation presented itself as a personal issue when one of the Church of Scotland missionaries, the Rev. Andrew Doig, was invited to represent African interests in the Federal Assembly. After much deliberation he accepted. He did this because he had been a member of the pre-Federation Legislative Council of Nyasaland and was known to have consistently opposed federation. As the Church had supported the Africans against the federation proposals, it was now important to continue to take the strain with them and work for their interests as a European. Further, only a known member of the Church could meet the leaders of African thought, who are within the Church, and help to lead them out of their despair and bitterness and keep hope alive within them. At the same time, only a European could get alongside European members of the Assembly and help them to realise what was happening among Africans.

Here surely the involvement of the Church in the sin of the world is seen without any doubt. The failure of the churches in South Africa to resolve their problems and the problems of their society means that the northern territories are infected. The failure of the churches in Britain so to interpret, persuade and educate public opinion that another way than forcible Federation could be found, has led to discouragement to the young Church in Nyasaland. And yet in all three countries there are those who are seeking to bear the burden redemptively so that God's grace and power may be seen to triumph over the foolishness and sinfulness of men.

The Mau Mau movement is but another and more terrible illustration of the same involvement. Jomo Kenyatta, one of the leaders of the movements which developed into the Mau Mau rising, was educated in a Christian school and further trained in Britain at the London School of Economics. Who knows how far his sense of injustice, of the wrongs done to his countrymen —exaggerated, but not without a basis of fact—may have been fostered by his Christian training and acquaintance with the Bible? How different might events have been if, when in England, he had come to know the live elements in the Christian Church, which might have shown him more positive ways for seeking to bring about social change?

It is also well known that the leading members of the Mau Mau were recruited from disaffected teachers who, being dismissed from mission schools, set up independent schools which became centres of revolutionary influence. Parodies of Christian hymns and Christian ceremonies were used to incite violence against the white man, as though taking the white man's medicine and using it to poison him.

The resistance of the convinced Christians among the Kikuyu, even to the point of martyrdom, has been one of the magnificent stories in the Church of this century. The Revival Movement, which has been at the heart of the resistance, has been described as "a return to the simplicity of apostolic faith in times of Apostacy." "Recognising no barriers but sin," it has been the means of reconciliation of man with God and man with man. It has brought together in Christian fellowship, based on the forgiveness of Christ, black and white, men of different races and tribes, men and women. But the Mau Mau troubles broke upon the movement before it had translated this experience into political or economic terms. It could provide the spirit which might accept change, but not the programme of change. Its love remained in personal terms and was not translated into justice. The relation between religion and politics has not been made and the result is suffering for the whole community.

In this responsibility, the European settlers and the Government are even more deeply implicated because of their greater opportunities and experience. It has been said that the proportion of faithful and believing Christians is probably greater among these European groups than among the Kikuyu—as indeed it should be. Among them too have been shining examples of Christian grace—some volunteers working in the detention camps for the rehabilitation of the Mau Mau are those who have suffered most at their hands, through the murder of members of their own family. But while we thank God for such courage, we remember also that the state of affairs has been aggravated over the years not so much by the grosser sins as by the sins of omission. Leakey points out in his books[1] that the Mau Mau movement could never have grown so strong if the European settlers and government officials had been more aware of African opinion, more sensitive to African grievances, well or ill founded, and more able to understand the language that was spoken among the servants in their own households.

In the Autumn of 1955, celebrations were held to mark the centenary of Livingstone's discovery of Victoria Falls. It is only

[1] *Understanding Mau Mau*, L. S. B. Leakey (Methuen); *The Mau Mau and the Kikuyu*, L. S. B. Leakey (Methuen).

a hundred years since he "opened up" Africa. In the same year the first All-Africa Christian Conference was held, called by the Lutheran World Federation, with representatives of other churches present as guests. It has been a century of unparalleled development and change in which Christian forces have played a remarkable part. The next century will show whether the Cross in Africa is to be the sign of agony or of triumph as well.

VII

"Lest the Cross of Christ be made void"

"Now I beseech you, brethren, through the name of our Lord Jesus Christ, that ye all speak the same thing and that there be no divisions among you; but that ye be perfected together in the same mind and in the same judgment. . . . Is Christ divided? Was Paul crucified for you? . . . For Christ sent me not to baptise but to preach the gospel; not in wisdom of words, lest the cross of Christ should be made void." (I Cor. 1: 10, 13, 17)

We are so used to the situation of a divided Church that we take it as normal. We have so been brought up on the stories of the great men of our own particular denomination that we are filled with party loyalty. We read the New Testament, and particularly the Epistles as if it were possible for all that is said about the Church to apply equally well to each of our divided churches. It does not easily occur to us, as it did to Paul, that, just as the lack of faith of the people of Jesus' own country prevented him from doing many mighty works there, so the lack of unity in the Church which is his Body can also prevent the saving power of the Cross from being effective.

This is a terrible thought, but it runs right through St. Paul's exhortations to the young Christian communities in Rome, Corinth, Philippi and Galatia. How are people to believe if the New Community called into being by the Spirit of God does not live by the Spirit of God? The unity of the Church was mainly threatened in four ways. First, as in Corinth, people were attaching themselves to leaders. Secondly, false apostles were "preaching another Jesus" (II Cor. 11) and leading astray the

Church founded by the apostles. Thirdly, personal disagreements arose, such as, apparently, between Euodia and Syntyche in the Philippian Church (Phil. 4: 2), and fourthly, major disagreements in the Church such as that over preaching to the Gentiles (Acts 11: 1-18) and circumcision as a condition of admission to the Christian Church (Galatians 5: 1-12).

In the face of all these divisions or threats of division, Paul appeals with all the energy of which he is capable that the Church will recognise that its life is in Christ and nowhere else, and that if it lives in him then there cannot and must not be division. For Paul unity is not a matter of good organisation, or of numerical strength in facing a non-Christian world. It is the nature of the Church and its life in Christ that is at stake.

ALL through the previous chapters, it has been clear that the task of the Church is one task—to make known the Gospel of Christ throughout the world and to work with Him for its salvation. Yet we seek to carry it out through our divided churches.

Everyone who knows the ABC of the ecumenical movement knows that its modern phase began with the World Missionary Conference in Edinburgh 1910. But that itself could not have happened unless before it there had already been much consultation among missionaries on "the field". "Inevitably, as missionaries moved into India, China, Japan, and the countries of Africa and Latin America, they encountered problems requiring joint consultation. Nearly always this meant sharing helpful information and providing mutual counsel. In a few cases it meant alleviating friction that arose when one society encroached on territory or appealed to converts of another."[1] The sense of unity and common purpose was strong enough among those who met together for friction to be smoothed out and the policy of "comity" to be evolved. This means an agreement between missions to respect each other's "territorial rights". If the S.P.G.

[1] Ecumenical Foundations, W. R. Hogg, p. 16.

is already at work in one area, the L.M.S. will go elsewhere rather than compete. It later led to agreements as to which body should enter new territory. It was obviously the only workable system among groups which respected each other, both to avoid friction and to extend rather than overlap. It worked fairly well so long as people stayed at home, though it was never all-embracing. The Roman Catholics are, of course, outside all co-operative work, and the Faith missions and others of the more independent groups have never "respected comity". There was in general an agreement between churches working in the country districts and those in the cities to which people went for work or study. This raised no major problems between churches (e.g. the English Free churches) where there were no barriers to communion. It was already more difficult where there were Anglicans involved. The weakness of the system has become clearer as the sense of our need of one another as Churches has become stronger. It was summed up by a young Lebanese Orthodox delegate to the Kottayam World Christian Youth Conference when she said, "It seems to me that for you Protestants, geography is more important than doctrine!" It was a working arrangement which left all difficult questions on one side. It broke down completely when populations began to shift.

We can be thankful that there was enough mutual trust and sense of common purpose among the early missionaries to establish as workable a system as comity. Today it is not only proving unworkable in such situations as the Kenya detention camps or the Malayan villages, where responsibility must be taken by the Christian community as a whole, but it is being felt to be theologically unsatisfactory. Do we really care so little about the fullness and richness of the Christian faith that it does not matter to us whether a man or a province or a nation so much as knows that there are other aspects of Christian life, faith or worship than those emphasised by the tradition to which he has been "allotted"? But the alternatives, up to recent times, have all looked as if they would lead to rivalry rather than to enrichment.

Edinburgh 1910, however, inaugurated a new era. Following up the Conference, Dr. John R. Mott, as Chairman of the Continuing Committee which later became the International Missionary Council, travelled widely throughout Asia, holding follow-up Conferences of Christian leaders, both national and missionary. He urged them to set up committees able to organise Christian co-operation on a national scale in evangelism, medicine, education and literature. These later became National Christian Councils and John R. Mott considered his share in their formation his first and his greatest contribution to the International Missionary Council.

If the slogan of the missionary consultations was "comity", that of the National Christian Councils was—and still is— co-operation. Increasingly led and staffed by nationals, they have made it possible, as the various missions acting independently could not, to think nationally and to meet new situations as they arose. They have been indispensable in all countries going through political change, for it is they alone who have been able to deal directly with Governments on questions of religious liberty, entrance of missionaries, etc. They have provided a regular meeting place for consultation between church leaders, especially as the churches become more and more indigenous. They have also greatly helped the younger churches to feel that they are active partners in a world Christian community and not merely at the receiving end of the missionary enterprise.

But increasingly it is being felt that co-operation is not enough, for it leaves the relations between churches unchanged.

As the Christian communities have grown up, small in numbers and with limited resources in leadership, they have failed to understand why they should be further weakened over against the non-Christian overwhelming majority, by division. In any land where Christians are a minority of perhaps 2 per cent their sense of fellowship with other Christians *must* be more important than difference in churchmanship. Yet when this difference separates them one from another at the Lord's Table it becomes tragic and unbearable. That something is radically wrong is borne in upon them even more forcibly when they read the New Testament and understand something of the New Community which is in Christ. No metaphor of regiments in one army or even branches of one tree is adequate to describe the "I in you and you in Me" which is Christ's way of speaking of the Body of which He is Head.

Out of this dissatisfaction has come a conviction that, however justified in the past, for the Church today, disunity is sin. This was forcibly expressed in the statement of the younger church leaders at Tambaram in 1938:—

"During the discussion it became abundantly clear that the divisions of Christendom were seen in their worst light in the mission field. Instances were cited by the representatives of the younger churches of disgraceful competition, wasteful overlapping, and of groups and individuals turned away from the Church because of the divisions within. Disunion is both a stumbling block to the faithful and a mockery to those without. We confess with shame that we ourselves have often been the cause of thus bringing dishonour to the religion of our Master. The representatives of the younger churches in this Section one and all gave expression to the passionate longing that exists in all countries for visible union of the churches."[1]

The Faith and Order Section of the World Council of Churches Assembly in 1954 also made a strong statement. It is significant that this time it is not only representatives of the younger churches but of the churches as a whole, who are speaking:—

"There is diversity which is not sinful but good, because it reflects both the diversities of gifts of the Spirit in the one body and diversities of creation by the one Creator. But when

[1] *The World Mission of the Church*, I.M.C. 1939, p. 155.

diversity disrupts the manifest unity of the Body, then it changes its quality and becomes sinful division. It is sinful because it obscures from men the sufficiency of Christ's atonement, inasmuch as the gospel of reconciliation is denied in the very lives of those who proclaim it."[1]

Of all the unions that have been accomplished in the last thirty years, and there have been many, far and away the most important is the Church of South India, because this is the first union of episcopal with non-episcopal churches. It is immensely important for Christian witness in South India, as it seeks to express the reality of the Church Universal in a South Indian setting. It is a great example and encouragement to other areas which are equally feeling that a new step must be taken. Schemes of union are now far advanced in Ceylon and North India, and the Moderator of the Church of South India visited Nigeria in 1955, sharing with the churches there the South Indian experience and helping them to formulate their own plans for union.

But more than all this, the Church of South India is a challenge to the "parent" churches of the West. The act of faith taken in September 1947 will only result in the addition of one more to the list of "denominations" unless the union there effected is the beginning of closer union between the churches which united to form the Church of South India. The Moderator of the Second Synod expressed this cogently when he said in 1951: "More and more it must become clear that it is not we in our union who are the anomaly, but the disunited churches here and abroad which still too largely look upon a divided Church as the normal condition of those who profess their faith in the same God, the same Saviour, the same Holy Spirit. It is not our uniting which needs to be justified, but their separation."[2]

It was for this reason that the reconsideration by the Convocations of the Church of England of relations with the Church

---

[1] Report of Faith and Order Section, W.C.C. Assembly 1954; *Evanston Speaks*, p. 22.

[2] Marcus Ward: *The Pilgrim Church*, p. 51.

of South India was awaited with such eager concern. There is cause for rejoicing that the Church of England acknowledges the Church of South India as a true Church. The Church of England has, however, never entered into full communion with any Church with a ministry, some of whom were not episcopally ordained. In that respect the C.S.I. does not create a precedent, and it was perhaps unreasonable to expect a change of policy. The situation is to be re-examined when the thirty year period of growing together is over.

Further, conversations which have been begun in England and Scotland between Episcopal and Presbyterian churches and which are foreseen between the Church of England and the Methodist Church, are the beginning of an answer to the question put to all divided churches by the Church of South India: "If it is possible for us to unite and for you to acknowledge us as a Church, is it possible for you to remain divided? Is this not to deny the Gospel of reconciliation which we preach?"

While we rejoice in the growing momentum of the movement for reunion which is evident in all parts of the world, we have also to take account of a contrary movement. While the major churches represented in the World Council of Churches (except the Orthodox, for reasons of their own ecclesiology) are drawing into closer relationships, there is at the same time a greatly increased missionary activity on the part of the multiplicity of sects who have never taken any part in co-operation or consultation either at home or abroad. Many of these are Pentecostal groups which present a problem to the more highly organised churches, for they frequently create division within a congregation already established. At the same time, they pose the question whether the churches are in fact "quenching the Spirit" and not allowing adequate expression for God's free Spirit, which may work in ways unfamiliar or uncongenial to their traditions. There have been encouraging signs that there is greater readiness on the part of churches and Pentecostal movements to talk together and listen to each other, so that at least the spirit of rivalry and distrust may be lessened and it may be that a fuller place may be given in the churches for groups which are conscious of the movement of the Spirit among them, without them having to separate themselves off.

Bodies like the Seventh Day Adventists and Jehovah's Witnesses create confusion because, while claiming to be Christian, their doctrines are at variance with orthodox Christian belief.

But there are also other forces at work which can only be called "false prophets", elements which for unworthy reasons are anxious to create division and to destroy the "growing together" of the churches. They foment dissension, give support to any dissatisfied element, and sow seeds of trouble by falsely representing facts. It is very hard for inexperienced Christians, zealous for truth, to resist propaganda when it is done in the Name of Christ, and for the Truth of the Word of God. But there is one test which is to be found in the Bible and which is a reliable guide: "God gathers, the enemies of God scatter." (cf. Matt. 12:30; John 10:12).[1]

There was a wonderful moment in the Festival of Faith presented at the Evanston Assembly. The story of our redemption was symbolically acted out as the great words of Scripture were read. It came to the founding of the Church, and from all sides of the vast stadium groups of men and women came together to form one "building", arms upraised as they gave glory to God. Then suddenly, fragments broke away and great jagged holes were left in what had been a unity. The "rending of the body", which is dissension, came home with startling clarity.

But, alas, the story is not all told when we have talked of relations between churches of different denominational or theological loyalties. The question of denying or affirming "the sufficiency of the atonement" comes right home into the life of

[1] cf. *The Fellowship of the Gospel*, Evangelical Alliance publication.

the congregation. A few years ago an international consultation of Christian youth leaders was held to consider the dilemma created for the Church by the large number of young people who leave the Church just at the time when they have made the solemn act of uniting themselves with it by Confirmation. Various criticisms of church life were considered and then the group reported the outcome of their common Bible study on I Cor. 12:—

"We realised that the Holy Spirit, under the form of love, is alone able to create a 'living together' in the midst of tensions and diversities. The tensions will not disappear, but the unity will be enriched by variety, not impoverished. We realised that, if only those individuals or groups live together who like each other, there is no need for the Spirit and no Spirit will be given. But if we accept the adventure of living together with those who differ from us, we must ask for the Spirit."[1]

The adventure of living together! The Church is not a social club or a society of the like-minded. It consists of those who have been "reconciled to God" by the Cross of Christ, and the sign of reconciliation with God is love of the brethren.

Somehow we have let this emphasis slip in our Western churches. If we disagree with the minister or have a quarrel with a fellow-member, there is always another church we can go to. It has been for the younger churches to remind us that the power of the Spirit of God to create unity *must* be demonstrated in the Church if it is to be believed by the world. Where Christian communities are small, these things are a matter of life or death. Here is a picture of recent experiences in a little Christian group in East Pakistan:—

"The year brought unprecedented problems in the life of the congregation; problems of living and working together as a small band of Christ's people set in a non-Christian area,

[1] Report of Youth Leaders' Consultation, Bossey 1952, W.C.C. Youth Department.

when the members are often of very different backgrounds and have no natural bonds of friendship or even liking between them. Indeed, it often appears that they have nothing whatever in common apart from their Christian faith, and on all other counts there is plenty of reason for antipathy and positive dislike. In a congregation in England, for example, even in a small one, it is usually possible for members to hide their antipathies if they so wish, and to escape from them in happier relationships with others whom they feel to be more congenial. In a small closely knit community such as the congregation at . . . there is no escape, no decent covering up, for all relationships, pleasant or unpleasant, lie open to the common gaze. A congregation either learns what it means to keep its life subservient to the mind and will of the Lord, and to depend upon the help and guidance of the Holy Spirit to create right relationships, or it soon ceases to exist as a Church of Christ. . . . Although on the basis of what seemed humanly possible and probable, there was often little hope of reconciliation, yet by the Spirit's help fellowship was not only restored but deepened by the dark experience it survived. Now . . . the congregation can gladly confess that God has made even the wrath of man to praise Him; that He has used the things which vexed them for their good and for his glory."[1]

No one who has read the life of Florence Allshorn, told by J. H. Oldham, will forget the incident at the beginning of Florence Allshorn's missionary work in Africa, where she was sent to live in an isolated station with an extremely difficult senior colleague:—

"I was young," she wrote, "and I was the eighth youngster who had been sent, none of whom had lasted for more than two years. I went down to seven stone and my spirit and soul wilted to the same degree. Then one day the old African matron came to see me when I was sitting on the verandah crying my eyes out. She sat at my feet and after a time she said: 'I have been on this station for fifteen years and I have

[1] B. Dawson in *Far Horizons* (Presbyterian Church of England), No. 72.

seen you come out, all of you, saying you have brought to us a Saviour, but I have never seen this situation saved yet'."[1]

Brought up short with a shock, she knew that everything depended upon showing that the love of Christ could triumph. It was a hard fight, but she won and "from that moment everything was changed." The atoning work of Christ was sufficient.

One of the saddest internal disputes in any church, and one which has been going on for over seventy years, is in the Syrian Orthodox Church of Malabar in South India. It is a dispute over the question of supreme authority in the Church, and has sapped spiritual and material resources, used up energy and brought the contending parties before the Hindu courts. But it has also caused great grief and concern to many of the younger members in this Church, who several years ago formed themselves into a Peace League to work for arbitration in a Christian spirit. A recent visitor to India, Secretary of the World Council of Churches Department of Faith and Order, describes a scene which he witnessed:—

"One of the large churches had been closed by court order for years. Before the locked doors of the church was a simple altar and over the large courtyard a covering of bamboo and palm. In one place sat the men who at that time were completing their 52nd day of fasting, being very thin, bearded, and some sickly. About 200 people, including many children, had gathered for evening worship with them. I spoke briefly on the text, 'Christ is our Peace,' and then joined in their form of Compline. . . . While some persons questioned whether the fasting could have further practical effect, none could fail to be impressed by these gaunt martyrs, who have been willing to go the bitterest way of the Cross for the sake of the unity of the Church. Inevitably I found myself being judged for the comparatively inexpensive and comfortable way in which I have been working for manifest unity."

Do many of us realise the spiritual issues which are involved

[1] Florence Allshorn, by J. H. Oldham, S.C.M. Press, p. 28.

GI

in division within the Church, or are we content to take an easy way? A recent notice in a Scottish paper told of a congregation which resolved to go out of existence rather than take part in a union which would mean leaving its church building. Did the people realise that they were thereby registering a defeat for the Spirit of God? If the Cross of Christ is not relevant to our ordering of Church affairs, can we expect other people to believe in its relevance for their lives?

This "adventure of living together" refers to even more than parties in the Church or personal likes and dislikes. It challenges all churches which have been prepared to come to terms with division also on the basis of national traditions or race or social status.

There are pieces of good news here and there to report. The Churches in India have taken over responsibility for caring for the British population in India and the Anglo-Indian community, both of which were largely cared for by establishment chaplaincies in the days of British India. The Government grants which supported them have entirely gone—they are now more obviously part of the Indian Church than they were before. In Nairobi, the union has taken place of the Overseas Presbytery of the Church of Scotland (of European congregations) with the Presbyterian Church of East Africa (largely African) and in this church is an Indian missionary appointed by the United Church of North India. Where one is aiming at a multi-racial society, it is surely a pre-requisite that there should be a multi-racial church.

Sometimes the barrier is not that of race but of language. It is easy to make this an excuse for separate organisation which can easily lead to a deeper sense of separation. That this need not happen is shown in Bombay. There the Methodist Episcopal Church of South-East Asia has twelve congregations, each worshipping in a different language, yet all consciously and actively part of the same church.

So with congregations or churches which tend to represent

one social group or one class interest. Only slowly is it dawning on us that each individual congregation, wherever it may be, must represent the Church in that place—the Church, and not the church of a particular school of thought, or the church of a social group, or a national culture. It is easy to rationalise and to justify "group" churches on the grounds that people are more likely to come if they meet the kind of people that they know or if the form of worship is familiar, or if they will not have their prejudices shocked. But are they not also equally likely to stay away because the Church seems to offer them nothing different from the world? The Evanston Section on Inter-group Relations spoke with its mind made up on this issue:—

"Racial and ethnic fear, hates and prejudices are more than social problems with whose existence we must reckon; they are sins against God and His commandments that the Gospel alone can cure."[1]

And again:—

"What is the Christian hope in this disunity? It is Jesus Christ, who revealed God as Father and who died for all men, reconciling them to God and to each other by the Cross. From every race and nation a new people of God is created, in which the power of the Spirit overcomes racial pride and fear. So far from being without hope or purpose, God's people now as new creatures are co-workers with Him, and are filled with joy and assured of His final victory."[2]

[1] Report of Section V, paragraph v; *Evanston Speaks*, p. 92.
[2] Report of Section V, paragraph ii; *Evanston Speaks*, p. 90.

VIII

"Let him take up his Cross"

"If any man would come after me, let him deny himself and take up his cross and follow me." (Matt. 16: 24-28)

If Peter was dismayed at the thought of suffering lying ahead for Jesus, it must have been even more of a shock to be told that those who followed Jesus must expect the same kind of life and death as Jesus Himself. "Remember the word that I said to you, 'A servant is not greater than his master. If they persecuted me, they will persecute you; if they keep my word, they will keep yours also'." (John 5: 20).

It is one of the most staggering things of the Gospels that Jesus shared everything with the disciples. He who was the Son of God became man so completely that he expected men to share with him both in his glory and his suffering. When he sent out the disciples on their first missionary journey, he gave them his authority to preach and heal and cleanse. When they acknowledged him as the Christ, he gave them the "keys of the kingdom of heaven". His life on earth was only a beginning. It was to continue in his disciples.

To call on his disciples to take up the Cross was not, as we often imply, to ask them to bear petty irritations cheerfully. Those who carried the Cross were slaves who had been caught in some act of rebellion against their Roman masters, and they carried it once only—to die on it. That Jesus understood this is clear from his next sentence: "For whoever would save his life will lose it, and whoever loses his life for my sake will find it."

The disciples were therefore so to live that they might at any time be taken to task for not giving their full allegiance to Caesar. Living in obedience to the will of God might as surely bring them to die by crucifixion as it had brought Jesus. According to tradition, this is exactly what happened, for of the three who were with Jesus at the Transfiguration, was not Peter said to have been crucified head down in Rome, and did not Andrew die on a diagonal cross in Asia Minor and was not John a political exile in the isle of Patmos?

But in the end of the day it was not the manner of death which was important but the manner of life. The Cross was not an end in itself but the consequence of following Jesus in daily obedience, wherever he might lead. And Jesus, even before His death, was able to assure them of what they could not see—that beyond the Cross lay the glory in which Christ reigns with God. To follow Christ, now as then, may be to go a way of human shame and apparent defeat, but it is to go in the confidence that he who "became obedient unto death, even death on a cross," has been exalted by God and that the day will come when "every tongue will confess that Jesus is Lord, to the glory of God the Father" (Phil. 2:9-11).

TO take up the Cross means to get involved with life where it counts.

Dietrich Bonhoeffer, the brilliant young German theologian, was on a lecture tour in America in 1939 when it was known that the situation in Germany was deteriorating. He was pressed on every hand by his American friends to stay in America and there take up some task suitable to his ecumenical spirit and his fine sensitivity to church life in other lands. But "he no longer saw any way of escape into some region of piety. He resolved to return to Germany and took one of the last boats sailing back to Germany before the war."[1] There he took a

[1] Letters and Papers from Prison, Dietrich Bonhoeffer, S.C.M. Press, Editor's Foreword, p. 9.

leading part in the work of the Confessing Church and in the resistance movement, and in April 1943 he was arrested. Yet, within the limits of a prison existence, he found himself brought into relation with people whom he could only have met formally or not at all if he had been free. He began to feel more intensely than before the separation that existed between the Church which he served and the people among whom he was forced to live. He took up the cross, not of his own suffering, but of an ineffective Church in a world without knowledge of God.

"You would be surprised and perhaps disturbed," he wrote to a friend, "if you knew how my ideas on theology are taking shape. . . . We are proceeding towards a time of no religion at all: men as they are now simply cannot be religious any more. . . . What does this mean for Christianity?

"I often ask myself why a Christian instinct draws me more to the religionless than to the religious, by which I do not mean with any intention of evangelising them, but rather, I might almost say, in 'brotherhood'. While I often shrink with religious people from speaking of God by name, with people who have no religion I am able on occasion to speak of God quite openly and, as it were, naturally. . . . Religious people speak of God when human perception is at an end, or when human resources fail. . . . Of necessity that can only go on until men can, by their own strength, push these borders a little further, so that God becomes superfluous. . . . I should like to speak of God not on the borders of life but at its centre, not in weakness but in strength, not therefore in man's suffering and death but in his life and prosperity. The Church stands not where human powers give out but in the centre of the village. . . . The outward aspect of this religionless Christianity, the form it takes, is something to which I am giving much thought, and I shall be writing to you about it again soon. . . ."[1]

These thoughts were never further developed, and a year later he was hanged in a German prison. But he had put into words

[1] Op. cit., pp. 122, 124.

seed thoughts which others have been able to take up and develop, which profoundly affect the thought of the Church in its relation with "cultural religion".

Throughout the war years Josef Hromadka of Czechoslovakia was a greatly loved professor at Princeton Theological Seminary, U.S.A. He too had many invitations to stay in America and help to interpret what was taking place in Continental theological thinking, thus building bridges between the churches. But, like Dr. Bonhoeffer, this would have seemed to Professor Hromadka to choose one's own way instead of to follow Christ. He went back to his country to take an active share in the struggle to found a new society. He accepted the Communist framework of society but maintained his freedom to speak to the leaders of his country of the higher justice and more demanding recognition of human rights which we learn in the Gospel. He has not always had the support of the church people at home. He was publicly attacked when he attended the Evanston Assembly, by Czechs who had emigrated rather than have anything to do with the new régime. But when he spoke to the Assembly on *The Church's Dependence on God and Its Independence from Man,* he spoke as one who had found a new depth of understanding of what it meant to obey the command, "Follow me!":—

"The Church is the body of Christ. As a communion of pilgrims walking in the steps of the Crucified and Risen Lord towards his ultimate victory, it cannot possibly desire an abstract independence from men. Jesus Christ has made himself the servant of men. He took upon himself the burden of his followers, disciples and adversaries. He did not come into the world with any idea of independence. He came to do his Father's will, to carry on a work of salvation, to rescue men, to suffer with them, to feed the hungry, to heal lepers and in the end, to die between thieves. What did his independence from men mean? Precisely this, that he had utterly forgotten himself, that he was absolutely free from the bonds of selfishness, that he transferred the centre of gravity of his life into his fellow men, his neighbours. . . . He was the Lord, but he proved to be the Lord exactly on the Cross, in the moment when all the misery of the world and of all men took hold of his human existence, when he was, literally, one of wretched, rejected sinners. . . .

"The freedom and independence of the Church is above all a majestic *yes* to the living God and to the man Jesus of Nazareth, the man in whom and through whom we come down to where human sinners live to be loved, awakened and uplifted through our message and self-forgetting service. . . . The Church has no right to yield to human standards, to political, social or cultural divisions, to stop before the barriers established by human traditions, prejudices, privileges, aspirations, snobbery and pride. . . ."[1]

In a rare and challenging way, Professor Hromadka has committed himself deeply to his own country and so drawn to himself the suspicions of those who are passionately anti-Communist. But he takes every opportunity of maintaining and strengthening links with Western countries and especially in tying closer the ties between churches—thus rousing the distrust of pro-Communists. The result *must* be suffering, but it also enables the Gospel to be heard in a new way by this politically dominated generation.

But war-time Germany and Communist Czechoslovakia may seem a far cry from a British town or village and the average reader may be feeling like the soldiers before John the Baptist: "And we, what do we do?" Very straightforward practical advice was given then, and perhaps the same is needed now.

The realism of Bonhoeffer and his desire to witness the true meeting of man with man in Christ, without sham or self-defence, challenges us all in our churches and our private lives. It makes us ask ourselves whether our circles need be so limited;

[1] Evanston Assembly papers: *The Church's Dependence on God and Independence from Man.*

whether our efforts at evangelism are rightly focussed or whether we are straining after the wrong things. Have we to learn still more from Christ the meaning of being truly human in our meeting with one another? Equally challenging is Hromadka's prayer for that independence from men which makes it possible to give ourselves in the loving service of our neighbour. This may involve not merely the neighbourly action quietly done, but the much more difficult public stand. It may demand the hum-drum work of political organisations, taking a share in local government—a task demanding self-denial in time and the use of leisure, requiring patience, charity and long-suffering in the highest measure which is all too easily left to those who are not "busy with church work".

If we are to add to these two a third challenge it is "to take up our cross *daily*", that is, in the present day world. Two words that characterise this world of today are *change* and *inter-relatedness*. Change: in all that the wars have left behind them—refugees seeking new countries, workers following new industries; changed tone and temper in international relations; and in the political status of many countries. And inter-relatedness because these things affect the lives of ordinary men and women to the ends of the earth. They determine social relations, dictate educational policy, and make common planning and action an unavoidable necessity.

To meet this situation, the churches have gradually built up their organs of common action. Internationally, the churches through the World Council of Churches and the International Missionary Council are geared to meet international emergencies, face international problems and bring the mind of the churches to bear on any new situation. Nationally also, Councils of Churches are tackling these questions together. But in many ways the churches in their separate and congregational life have not yet seen the consequences for themselves in the organs they have created. Who is to take action, for example, when a group of

Jamaicans (Colonial Missions) or African students (Foreign Missions) move into an industrial area (Home Missions) and have trouble over housing or employment (Social Action)? Is the local Christian community ready to take concerted action or does it fall between all stools?

The growth of churches established by missionary enterprise and their increasing autonomy means that we now have to think in new terms of inter-church relations on a world scale, rather than of any one church's Foreign Mission. Denominational foreign missionary societies still flourish and will continue to do so by reason of their long experience and special knowledge of their areas. But personnel is increasingly being recruited from more than one church or one nation. While this has long been the case in certain specialised institutions like Vellore Hospital in South India or the Madras Christian Colleges, it is more remarkable where it directly affects the life of the Church. Yet this is increasingly happening. In Indonesia, German, Dutch, American and Indian missionaries are all working in the independent Batak Church. In Nigeria, missionaries of the Canadian Presbyterian Church are coming in to strengthen work in which the Church of England, the Church of Scotland and the Methodists all share.

Theological training abroad is now increasingly being done on a united basis so that it begins to put questions to the churches which send missionaries. Is a church whose ministers have been trained in fellowship with those of other traditions likely to welcome men from this country whose theological education has been entirely within the "ethos" of one denomination?

Missionary service itself is rapidly changing character, not only because of Government restrictions on missionary entry, or on Christian teaching in schools, but also because of the rapid growth of educational and medical services in many countries. These things were previously largely in the hands of missions, but are now increasingly the concern of Governments or independent Boards. Help is now being sought also for technological and scientific development, opening up new areas of international association. The Africa Committee of a British Church recently stated:—

"The Committee had been impressed by the number of appointments urgently required for which the Churches and Missions shared responsibility, though these posts might not be filled by missionaries in the traditional sense. There were many vacancies for teachers advertised by the Overseas Appointments Bureau, not only in the Board of Governors Institutions associated with our own missions in Kenya and the Gold Coast, but in co-operative work where the staffing was dependent on the goodwill and efforts of the supporting missions even though the appointments were not offered on the usual missionary terms. There were also the appeals of the British Council of Churches and the World Council of Churches for work in the Kenya Rehabilitation Camps and the needs of the Free Church on the Copper Belt."[1]

This broadening of the basis affects recruits as well as Mission Boards. It means that men and women are needed for service who can work in teams with people of other races and nationalities, and other denominations than their own. It is not so much the spirit of the individual pioneer that is required as imagination, adaptability, the power to interpret and pass on experience and the willingness to train others rather than to do all the work oneself.

It also means that men and women with specialist knowledge are needed who are willing to serve, perhaps for a limited time, and can train others either "on the job" or in the universities. Some of these jobs carry high salaries and a good deal of prestige. They require men and women with just as great a sense of Christian vocation as those who go in normal missionary

[1] Minutes of the Church of Scotland Foreign Missions Committee, October 18th, 1955.

service. For them the cross may be in having to resist the temptations which salary and position bring, being willing to associate with the national, rather than the "white" church; using their leisure time in ways which make for fellowship with the people of the country rather than create barriers—thereby possibly finding themselves out of step with some of their colleagues. There is a real call for discipline and self-denial if a tradition of public service is to be built up which is acceptable to the new leadership of independent countries and is appropriate to the conditions and best interests of the country.

On the other hand, it may be a form of self-denial and cross-bearing to forego the high salaries and good conditions of Government jobs or of those in international agencies and to serve within the less materially attractive conditions of missionary appointments. What is lost materially may be more than made up in the sense of being allowed to take a share in the Christian enterprise of a new Church. It will not be without pain, for, though the churches cry out for help from abroad, they do not always know how to use it most effectively. Tensions and frustrations are part of the growing pains of a new relationship. It demands self-denial in more ways than in leaving home and country. But to withhold help now, which is what the shortage of recruits involves, is almost to push these churches into nationalist self-sufficiency and to deny in practice the reality of the Universal Church in which, when one member suffers or is in need, all the members suffer with it.

It is remarkable to find how frequently today public leaders in India quote the "missionary spirit" as an example of the disinterested service which they desire their own people to emulate. In countries where there are not enough doctors, teachers, technicians to meet the need, it is obviously a temptation to take the job which provides the best conditions for professional work as well as for living. It is no less a sacrifice for an Indian doctor to go to work in a village clinic than for a doctor from the West. If the "missionary spirit" is a Christian rather than a "foreign" characteristic, it must be carried on by the Church and not merely by the foreign missionary. But that does not mean that the Church to which it is handed over is to be left. We are only at the beginning of understanding the meaning of partnership in the world-wide Church. To cut ourselves or any Church off from the life of the whole would be a disaster.

There are new forms of work, no less "missionary" for not having the element of direct dealing with people. Why should it be considered a more direct form of service to teach a class of children than to prepare a good curriculum which others may use, or to tell a story to village women, rather than to edit a magazine which thousands might read? Yet the spread of Christian literature is being handicapped by lack of skilled writers. Many people must be holding back their service because they are still imagining the work of the Church overseas in last-century terms.

There are also widening forms of service being asked of the churches, not foreseen in earlier days when missionary budgets were drawn up, or not able to be met by the traditional channels. "War, political developments, the severance of ties with the West and the loss of former resources have placed severe and often crippling burdens upon many churches in Asia and Africa. This is all the more serious since these churches are now confronted with the overwhelming spiritual and social tasks which grow out of the revolutionary changes taking place in their countries. What is called for is inter-church aid on an ecumenical basis." This quotation comes from a report of the Inter-Church Aid Division of the World Council of Churches, headed *World Need and Strategy in 1955-56* with special reference to Asia and Africa. It marks the beginning of a new stage in Christian solidarity on a world scale, for it aims to strengthen the churches *for service* to the communities in which they are placed. Consulting together, the churches have been led "to a concern for the strengthening and renewal of church life in all the continents, and to a wider ministry to human need throughout the world."

The churches have been asked to list their most urgent needs unmet by regular church and mission programmes. In some cases these arise out of disasters such as war in Korea and famine or flood in India. In Korea, it has been possible to send staff with experience of the post-war refugee situation in Central Europe to help and guide the churches and Christian organisations in the tremendous task of caring for widows and orphans, in setting up workshops where amputees learn to make their own artificial limbs, and in other ways helping life to move again. Malaya has now asked for the accumulated experience of Europe and Korea to be made available for them as they try to face the demands of the new villages not only for evangelism but also for social organisation.

In India it is probably little known how far food supplies sent to famine areas by bodies like UNICEF travel through Christian agencies—nor how far churches themselves have been sending material aid. The American churches obtained vast supplies of surplus food through a Share Our Surplus campaign. This was offered to the World Council of Churches so that the distribution would not be associated with American policies and also so that those who would benefit should have a share in determining policy.

Apart from emergency help to meet disasters, it is interesting to see the kind of help for which the churches themselves ask. Indonesia asks first for scholarships to help train teachers, doctors and nurses. Funds are needed to help re-settle refugees. A rural reconstruction centre for training young farmers is another need. Surprisingly often, from other countries too, the request is for people to initiate self-help projects rather than for materials or money.

In all these new developments and needs it is easy to overlook the missionary societies who have constantly to re-think their function in the rapidly changing conditions, and to provide the workers demanded by new types of work. For generations they have borne the brunt of missionary responsibility in their own countries, often when their churches have been asleep to their world-wide obligation. Never have they had enough margin in missionary workers or money to allow much flexibility. In the post-war years they have been strained to the utmost to keep existing work going and to respond to the requests which the Churches overseas have put to them. They are equally under the Cross with their partners in the lands in which they work, and it is perilously fashionable to make them the scapegoat for all that does not go according to expectations. It is easy to assume that the Young Churches are always right and the sending Churches wrong. The trouble is that both are "partners in obedience" and sometimes in disobedience. A new vision of world mission is emerging, in which all differences of race, nation, missionary or national, older or younger churches, are being surmounted in our common membership of Christ, and in our partnership in His Mission to the world "all are new men in Christ Jesus".

Finally, this theme of "change" and "inter-relatedness" comes home to the life of every local church. "I'm fed up with this co-operation. For heaven's sake leave me alone to get on with my own job!" This cry of impatience with new ways is quoted from the Christian News Bulletin of Ceylon, but it has a universal ring about it. And the comment has universal application too: —

"... No unity, and no scheme for union and no prayers for the union of the churches have any meaning at all unless it is involving me and my neighbour. Our unity has got to have its setting in the life of the Christian in the congregation rather than in the representative in the committee room. It must involve him in an act of love, rather than in assent to a proposition. The act of love may be the extra trouble involved in making the necessary arrangements for people of another denomination to come to our Conference. It may be making the mental effort to understand the other man's point of view; it will certainly involve suffering fools gladly. We try to avoid all these things when we can, but there will be no church unity until we have taken up the cross of costly charity and repentance."

These are critical days for the Church in Africa, in Asia, but in this country too. It is possible even for a Church to miss the day of its visitation, to refuse the act of obedience to which it is called. But Jesus' call to his disciples still stands: "Let him deny himself and take up his cross *daily* and follow me." It is not enough to have a record of past achievement in missionary service or past devotion to the cause of Christ or past self-sacrifice for the sake of unity and concord. It is *now* that we are called to follow Christ, with the prayer that he may not be ashamed to acknowledge us before the Father and that we may be present when he brings in his Kingdom.

EPILOGUE

"The Fellowship of His Sufferings"
(Phil. 3 : 10)

The accent in the foregoing chapters has been largely on the problems the Church is facing as she tries to be faithful to her task at a time when the whole world is changing. It is a time of the shaking of much that had been thought of as fundamental, a time when much is called in question that had become well-established, when there is the discomfort entailed by radical change and the necessity of finding new ways to meet it. But is this the Cross? "Real suffering," said Bonhoeffer, after eighteen months in prison, "must be quite a different matter."[1] And Jesus said, "If any man would come after me, let him deny himself." In other words, the problems of adjustment to new conditions are nothing which we should take with resentment, or allow as an excuse for self-pity. They are part of the discipline of making an instrument fit for its purpose. The condition of cross-bearing is that we should first die to self-concern—as individuals or as churches.

There are churches which are being called upon to bear much more acute suffering, where every effort is being made to stamp the life out of the Church and reduce it to ineffectiveness. For all such there is the comfort that persecution was foreseen by Christ. In fact he promised that persecution on his account would bring with it its own blessing as well as reward in heaven (Matt. 5 : 11-12). Those who are enduring such persecution can vouch that He is true to his promise.

[1] Letters from Prison, p. 110.

But the suffering of which Paul writes in Philippians and elsewhere is not our's but Christ's. It is the suffering, or the trials or afflictions which come to us when we try to enter into Christ's longing for the salvation of the world. It is the "hunger and thirst after righteousness" which will never be satisfied until the whole world comes to the feet of Christ, and which therefore never allows us to live in complacency or at ease. "Jesus will be in agony till the end of the world," wrote Pascal, "we must not sleep all that time." And Bonhoeffer echoed the same thought when he wrote in his poem *Christians and Unbelievers*: "Christians stand by God in his hour of grieving."[1] All men go to God in their need. He gives himself to all men, but "Christians stand by God". That is what above all distinguishes them from others.

This kind of suffering does not lead to despair, nor to the isolation of self-pity. Rather it leads into the heart of that fellowship with God and with other men which is the meaning of being "in Christ". "Blessed be God," says Paul, ". . . who comforts us in all our affliction, so that we may be able to comfort those who are in any affliction" (II Cor. 1: 3-4), and "I consider that the sufferings of this present time are not worth comparing with the glory that is to be revealed to us" (Rom. 8:18).

We have kept our eyes on the side of the Cross where Christ hangs, a revelation to all men of man's sin and God's love. We can only endure to be there, because it was there that God wrought his mighty work in raising Christ from the dead and making him to sit at his right hand. The other side of the Cross, where Christ reigns in glory, is the assurance and the hope by which the Church lives.

[1] Op. cit., p. 166.